# European Migration Policies in Flux

D1319257

# CHATHAM HOUSE PAPERS

The Royal Institute of International Affairs, at Chatham House in London, has provided an independent forum for discussion and debate on current international issues for over eighty years. Its resident research fellows, specialized information resources and range of publications, conferences and meetings span the fields of international politics, economics and security. The Institute is independent of government and other vested interests.

Chatham House Papers address contemporary issues of intellectual importance in a scholarly yet accessible way. In preparing the papers, authors are advised by a study group of experts convened by the RIIA, and publication of a paper indicates that the Institute regards it as an authoritative contribution to the public debate. The RIIA is, however, precluded by its Charter from having an institutional view. Opinions expressed in this publication are the responsibility of the author.

# European Migration Policies in Flux

## Changing Patterns of Inclusion and Exclusion

## Christina Boswell

THE ROYAL INSTITUTE OF INTERNATIONAL AFFAIRS | European Programme

Blackwell Publishing

The Royal Institute of International Affairs
Chatham House
10 St James's Square
London SW1Y 4LE
http://www.riia.org
(Charity Registration No: 208223)

Blackwell Publishing Ltd
350 Main Street, Malden, MA 02148-5018, USA
108 Cowley Road, Oxford OX4 1JF, UK
550 Swanston Street, Carlton South, Melbourne, Victoria 3053, Australia
Kurfürstendamm 57, 10707 Berlin, Germany

First published 2003 by Blackwell Publishing Ltd

Reprinted 2005

*Library of Congress Cataloging-in-Publication Data has been applied for*

ISBN 1-4051-0295-0 (hardback); ISBN 1-4051-0296-9 (paperback)

*A catalogue record for this title is available from the British Library.*

Set in 10.5 on 13 pt Caslon with Stone Sans display
By Koinonia, Manchester

For further information on
Blackwell Publishing, visit our website:
http://www.blackwellpublishing.com

# Contents

# Contents

Contents

# Acknowledgments

Many people contributed in one way or another to the writing of this book. My thanks go to Julie Smith, Head of the European Programme at Chatham House, for her support throughout the project, and her detailed comments on the draft. She and also Kim Mitchell did a meticulous job in editing the book. Tina Loewe acted as research assistant for chapters 2 and 3, and helped me with Italian texts. Ferruccio Pastore helped to clarify recent Italian legislation for me, and Georg Classen contributed his insights on aspects of German asylum law. Omar Feraboldi shared his vast knowledge of and insight into Italian politics and the Berlusconi phenomenon. Eleanore Kofman, Eiko Thielemann, Beth Ginsburg, Yongmi Schibel, Andrew Geddes, Jonathan King and Rachel Prime provided very useful comments on the draft. It goes without saying that none of the above-mentioned bear any responsibility for mistakes or omissions in the book.

I wish to give especial thanks to the Beryl Le Poer Power Trust for sponsoring this project at the European Programme of the Royal Institute of International Affairs. Its grant enabled us to fund research, editorial costs, travel and the organization of a study group to discuss the manuscript. I also owe a debt of gratitude to the European Commission's Marie Curie Fellowship Scheme, which provided funding for a two-year research project in Hamburg on EU responses to international migration.

*July 2003*                                                                 C.B.

# About the author

Dr Christina Boswell is an Associate Fellow of the Royal Institute of International Affairs, and Senior Researcher at the Migration Research Group, Hamburg Institute of International Economics. She previously worked as a policy research consultant for the UN Refugee Agency. Her research focuses on European immigration and refugee policy. Her publications include *EU Enlargement: What are the Prospects for East-West Migration?* (RIIA, 2000).

# Introduction

European migration policies are in a period of flux. After almost three decades of measures designed to restrict the rights of immigrants, many states are once again beginning to acknowledge the need for additional immigration. Labour migrants are required to fill gaps in labour markets, not only in specialized sectors such as information technology or health care, but also in low-skilled occupations including manufacturing, agriculture and catering. Moreover, many experts have argued that increasing numbers of migrants will be needed to offset the impact of ageing populations. As the proportion of the working population decreases in western Europe, there will be growing gaps in the labour supply and rising public spending costs. Increased labour migration is seen by many as one important means of filling these labour gaps and helping to meet rising health and welfare costs.[1]

However, the new liberalizing tendency is far from uncontested. It comes at a time of profound public anxiety over the social, economic and security impacts of migration and refugee flows. Growing levels of illegal migration and migrant-trafficking as well as perceived linkages between migration and terrorism have triggered doubts about the capacity of states to protect their citizens from outsiders. These fears have been fed over the past decade by a persistently anti-asylum and anti-illegal migration discourse in the media and in public debate. They have also been exploited by far-right parties, keen to mobilize support on an anti-immigrant platform. The electoral success of right-wing populist parties in France, Italy, the Netherlands, Denmark and Austria attest to the effectiveness of such policies in generating public support.

At the same time, many states have also had growing doubts about the effectiveness of strategies for integrating resident minority groups. Over the past few years, France, the United Kingdom and Germany have all experienced heated and highly sensitive debates about multiculturalism and self-

1

identity. Concerns about integration have been exacerbated by fears about Islamic fundamentalism in the wake of the 11 September 2001 attacks on the United States. Again, these issues have been taken up by both far-right and centrist political parties, to justify continued or more stringent restrictions on migration.

This anti-immigrant hostility is not necessarily targeted at labour migrants as such. Much of the public discourse on the costs of migration in west European countries has focused on problems of abuse of asylum systems, as well as on questions of illegal entry and irregular employment. Labour migrants who have entered legally and are in possession of regular work permits have rarely been singled out as the central target of public hostility. Nonetheless, the distinctions between these categories of migrants – illegal immigrants, asylum-seekers, recognized refugees, long-term residents and ethnic minority groups, and regular labour migrants – are often blurred in the public debate.[2] Thus moves to liberalize certain types of labour migration may well spark forms of anti-immigrant sentiment which do not differentiate between humanitarian or economic migrants or between those with legal or illegal status. Moreover, more general concerns about the impact of migration on collective identity, and doubts about whether immigrants are willing or able to integrate, are often targeted at all categories of migrants, regardless of their legal status or purpose of stay.

This apparent tension between the increasing demand for labour migration and public hostility to immigration raises two major questions for the future of west European migration policies. The first is how far we can expect more liberal labour migration policies to emerge and to be politically sustainable. While centre-left and liberal parties, business and many lobby groups remain committed to recruiting additional labour migrants, large sections of public opinion and right-wing political parties remain sceptical or overtly hostile to such approaches. Which sets of interests are likely to prevail and which factors will determine this? How far will the outcome diverge between different west European states?

The second question concerns how such policies are likely to affect other groups of migrants and refugees. Where more liberal labour migration policies do emerge, how, if at all, will they affect provisions for other categories of migrants – refugees, asylum-seekers, illegal immigrants and those seeking to join their families in west European states? Some have argued that the liberalization of labour migration policies will have a generally benign impact on attitudes towards these other groups. However, given the highly politicized nature of migration issues, political parties may be keen to continue to mobilize electoral support by promising more restrictive measures for these categories. Which factors will influence the treatment of different groups of migrants and refugees, and how will this vary between states?

If we are to make any headway in addressing these two sets of questions, we need to have some understanding of the factors determining migration policies. What domestic and international factors shape these policies in west European states? Policy-making in this area has become far more complex and contested since the early 1970s. Until then, most west European states followed a largely clientelist and elite-led pattern of policy formation: migration policies were determined predominantly by considerations of labour needs and foreign policy priorities. Political elites in European immigration countries such as Germany, France, Belgium, the Netherlands and Switzerland largely concurred on the economic case for labour migration, while various international political commitments – relations with former colonies or Cold War politics – influenced a relatively generous entry policy for the nationals of certain countries. From the 1970s onwards, however, migration issues increasingly became the subject of party political debate. This was partly a result of the growing perception among electorates that immigration could have multiple impacts on their societies – not just on their economies and labour markets but also on welfare, social services and social cohesion. Political parties quickly discovered that these concerns provided excellent material for political mobilization.

The increased politicization of migration issues has undoubtedly encouraged more restrictive policies in west European states. But it has in turn generated resistance from a number of other organized interests in European societies. Although few mainstream political parties have dared to risk alienating electorates by advocating liberal immigration and asylum policies, business lobbies have continued to press for more flexible provisions for recruiting migrant labour. Trade unions have also increasingly allied themselves with legal migrant workers, mainly to protect their members from competition from irregular migrant labour.[3] Meanwhile, human rights and refugee groups have expanded their lobbying activities on behalf of asylum-seekers and refugees.

These organized interests are not the only source of pressure to liberalize migration policies. West European governments have also had to face a number of more structural constraints on their attempts to restrict migration. One of these emanates from liberal democratic institutions: constitutional provisions, the courts and well-entrenched liberal bureaucratic cultures have in different ways impeded the introduction of policies which would undermine the basic rights of migrants and refugees. Another constraint stems from concerns about inter-ethnic relations, particularly where minority groups have been naturalized and have extensive political rights. The fear that exclusionary migration policies could jeopardize inter-ethnic relations may not have stopped governments from introducing restrictive entry policies, but it has forced them to be more careful about ensuring that policies towards migrants and refugees already resident are not overtly discriminatory. International commitments to human rights and refugee law, relations with sending countries and the process of EU harmonization have also in some ways acted as a constraint on domestic policies (although, as Chapter 5 shows, EU cooperation has also created new opportunities for restriction).

These various forms of constraints on domestic migration policies are not equally acknowledged by all sections of society or all political parties. Migration policy issues display an uncanny ability to trigger highly emotive and often ill-informed debates, and to generate often unfeasible political demands. One reason for this is the continued electoral incentive for more populist political actors to disregard the liberal democratic and international constraints mentioned above. Right-wing populist parties in Italy, the Netherlands, Germany and France have paid little heed to international or domestic human rights provisions, to the concerns of ethnic minority groups or to the requirements of EU cooperation. At least while such parties remain in opposition, they are relatively free to advance agendas which do not conform to domestic and international liberal and human rights standards. This has created what I term the 'populist gap': a gap between what can feasibly be done to restrict migration in liberal democracies and the often unrealistic and ethically unacceptable demands of populist politics. The 'populist gap' often pressures mainstream parties into embracing more radically restrictive measures in order to compete for electoral support.

A second, perhaps even more important reason for the emotive character of the debate relates to the way in which migration issues have become what Ulrich Beck has termed a 'lightning rod' for other diffuse social and economic anxieties.[4] Migration appears to offer a clear way of articulating ill-defined concerns about employment, welfare state reforms, education, criminality, national security and declining social homogeneity. It follows that proposals for more draconian migration policy measures provide a way of reassuring anxious electorates that the sources of these concerns can and will be addressed.

## PATTERNS OF INCLUSION AND EXCLUSION

Nevertheless, despite strong resistance to more liberal migration policies, it is not necessarily the case that labour migration reforms will be blocked. Growing gaps in labour markets and demographic constraints in the coming years are likely to place governments under enormous pressure to expand possibilities for labour migration. In fact, this configuration of pro- and anti-immigration interests could logically result in one of three scenarios.

The first is one in which no liberalizing reforms emerge at all. Anti-immigrant mobilization would continue to block a pro-business, reformist agenda, despite the negative repercussions on economic performance and welfare provisions. Such a policy is unlikely to be sustainable for long if labour shortages are patently crippling the economy. As we shall see, however, such a scenario may be compatible with toleration of large-scale illegal labour, which would substitute for an official recruitment policy.

Under the second scenario, liberalizing reforms would emerge, but without any significant impact on other areas of migration policy. In other words, the inclusion of economic migrants would not generate a move to exclude other migrant groups. It might even have a positive knock-on effect on other types of migrants and refugees, creating a generally positive climate towards them. This could be a plausible scenario if migration politics were to become less politicized in the coming years. However, there is little to suggest this will be the case: political parties continue to have incentives to mobilize support on migration issues, and the sorts of anxieties that generate anti-immigrant sentiment are, if anything, likely to increase in coming years. It is therefore difficult to imagine that such liberalization would take place in a context in which migration issues have become uncontested.

The third scenario is one in which migration reforms do emerge, but with a substantial impact on policy towards, and the treatment of, other categories of migrants. The thesis here is that economic and demographic pressures are not likely to instigate an undifferentiated shift towards more liberal migration policies. Instead, we are more likely to see a change in patterns of inclusion and exclusion. As it becomes imperative to recruit and incorporate economically beneficial groups of migrants into west European societies, other groups of non-economically beneficial migrants may well become the target of restrictive measures. Under this scenario, elite consensus on the need for economic migration will effectively remove the question of labour migration from the mainstream party political debate. But despite this new inclusion of labour migrants, the incentives for mobilizing support for the restriction of other types of immigration would continue unabated. Exclusionary rhetoric and policy proposals would be shifted more than ever onto those who are not considered to be economically productive or who are seen to create problems of migration control: asylum-seekers, illegal migrants and, in some countries, perhaps even long-term residents and ethnic minority groups.

The precise contours of these patterns of inclusion and exclusion may well vary from country to country. This will depend partly on what one could term 'ideologies of migration': patterns of political and social thought which shape thinking on a range of questions linked to migration, such as concepts of citizenship and belonging, rights and responsibilities of members, and obligations towards non-members. These ideologies of migration delimit the range of legitimate and feasible responses to migration in west European societies. Thus, for example, a civic republican concept of membership may dictate different criteria for inclusion and exclusion from a multiculturalist or an ethnocentric one.[5] Likewise, a strong tradition of economic liberalism may have fewer problems in incorporating labour migrants than a more welfare protectionist social model, and a more security-dominated discourse may be more prone to exclude illegal entrants and asylum-seekers, rather than resident ethnic groups and legal immigrants. Such ideologies of migration can, of course, change over time, and the imperative to justify additional labour migration may well influence which ones come to the fore in the coming years.

Patterns of exclusion will also depend on the types of domestic and international constraints mentioned above: the strength of different pro-refugee and pro-migrant lobby groups, constitutional and judicial checks, social partners and patterns of managing inter-ethnic relations. These ideological, political and institutional factors may therefore produce quite divergent discourses on inclusion and exclusion in different European states.

In order to understand these patterns of inclusion and exclusion in migration policy, we need to look in some detail at individual countries – not just at their legislation but also at their party politics, political institutions, ideologies of migration and popular discourse on immigration. The bulk of the empirical analysis in this book therefore focuses on three countries – Germany, Italy and the UK. Germany and the UK are classic postwar European receiving countries, although each has handled migration in a rather different way. Italy, by contrast, is a 'new' migration country, recently hit by a major political crisis, and has yet to achieve a 'settled culture' on migration.[6] All three have made moves to liberalize aspects of their labour migration policy. These moves have been the object of elite consensus in the UK, but probably at the expense of a crackdown on other groups, especially illegal migrants and asylum-seekers. In Germany, Chancellor Schröder's attempts at liberalization have aroused considerable resistance from the main opposition parties, and the future direction of this approach remains in the balance. Efforts by the left at reform in Italy in the 1990s were aborted by the right-wing coalition government that came to power in 2001. Each of these three countries therefore displays a different balance of pro- and anti-labour migration forces, reflecting quite divergent ideologies of migration, institutional structures and party political dynamics. They provide excellent cases for testing the three scenarios mentioned above: blocked reform, liberalization across the board, and new patterns of inclusion and exclusion.

## OUTLINE OF THE BOOK

The book starts by setting the historical scene for explaining current migration policies in western Europe. Chapter 1 maps out the main determinants of migration policies in Europe, examining how these have shaped different policy responses since the end of the Second World War. It explains how and why policy responses became so politicized in the 1970s, describing the breakdown in elite consensus, new patterns of electoral mobilization around migration issues, and the increasingly emotive treatment of migration questions in public debate. These developments have profoundly altered public debate and decision-making on migration issues in most west European receiving states.

Amid this highly charged policy debate comes the new challenge of rising demand for labour migration. Chapter 2 looks at the sources of this labour demand and how it has prompted some governments to liberalize certain aspects of their labour migration policies. Thus far the impetus has come mainly from centre-left governments, influenced by business lobbies and in some cases public-sector labour shortages, as well as by arguments about the need to attract new skills in the knowledge-based economy.

These so far relatively modest attempts at liberalization have met with resistance from different quarters and on different grounds. Some have criticized them as posing a threat to the jobs of indigenous workers. Others have been concerned about an apparent threat to cultural identity posed by additional immigration. A third, related line of argument has linked increased migration to problems of security, criminality or terrorism. How influential are these arguments, and what impact will they have on the liberalizing agenda? Or, to return to the three scenarios mentioned above, will such resistance block reforms entirely? Will it be trumped by more rational economic arguments? Or will it influence a shift in patterns of inclusion and exclusion?

Chapters 3 and 4 discuss these questions, focusing on two major issues of controversy in migration policy: responses to newcomers and migration management (often termed 'immigration policy'), and the integration of long-term residents and ethnic minorities (so-called 'immigrant policy').[7]

Chapter 3 looks at recent debates on the problem of control of new entrants, particularly asylum-seekers and illegal immigrants. Both groups have been the subject of increasingly restrictive measures since the 1980s and of a discourse linking them to problems of control and security, and of abuse of welfare systems. The chapter considers how far such discourse will impact on arguments for and against labour migration. In cases where more liberal labour migration policies have emerged, it examines how these will affect the treatment of these groups. Will illegal immigrants and asylum-seekers benefit from new labour migration policies or will they fall victim to new or reinforced patterns of exclusion?

Chapter 4 deals with the issue of immigrant integration, which has recently come to the fore as a major policy challenge in many west European states. In part this reflects the very real problems of incorporating ethnic minority groups. Integration has also become a symbolic issue, however, channelling a range of other concerns about collective identity and security. The chapter considers how far concerns about failed integration will influence the labour migration agenda. It discusses whether such concerns could block the emergence of more liberal policies, or whether they might lead instead to a much-needed rethinking of models of integration.

Chapter 5 looks at the international context of west European migration policy. It considers how far forms of regional, international and bilateral cooperation can contribute to addressing deficiencies in domestic migration policies. The chapter questions whether or not cooperation on migration management, burden-sharing and prevention have helped to address public anxieties about immigration; and, if they have, whether international cooperation could provide a partial solution to domestic conflicts over labour migration.

# 1

# *The evolution of postwar European migration policies*

Migration and refugee policy is one of the most contested political issues in western Europe today. It is frequently a central theme in local and general elections, and has been the key campaigning issue for an increasingly strong far right in many states. But the politicization of migration issues is a relatively recent occurrence in most countries. In the three decades after the Second World War, migration and refugee issues received little attention in public debates.

This was not because the level of immigration flows was lower than it is today. In fact, most west European countries recruited large numbers of immigrants in the late 1950s and the 1960s, mainly for labour purposes. The main difference was that immigration policies in this era were almost exclusively determined by political elites and their social partners, as a function of labour requirements or international relations. The recruitment of labour migrants in most continental west European countries was agreed upon by labour ministries, employers and trade unions, conforming to an essentially clientelist model of policy-making.[1] Policy on refugees, meanwhile, was very much shaped by the exigencies of Cold War international politics and the potent ideological symbolism of granting asylum to those fleeing communist states. Former colonial powers such as the UK, France and the Netherlands were also highly influenced by special ties with African, Caribbean and Asian countries in deciding rules on immigration. In most cases, migration and refugee policy was made with relatively little party political debate.

As migration and asylum issues became increasingly politicized in the 1970s and 1980s, this form of elite policy-making was no longer possible. Immigration began to be perceived as impacting on a range of critical social questions: unemployment, the welfare state, cultural identity, and even public order. Increasing concerns about the impact of immigration were partly a function of changes in the scale and composition of flows. This period saw larger numbers of immigrants and asylum-seekers arriving from developing countries, as well as an increased proportion of women, children and old people, who required more extensive state engagement in providing welfare and social assistance. Patterns of flows were also changing, generating concerns about controlling illegal flows and limiting abuse of asylum systems and possibilities for family reunion. Yet this growing anxiety about immigration was also a function of broader socio-economic changes linked to globalization and the changing role of the state. Insecurities about employment, welfare state reform and collective identity were readily channelled into concerns about immigration. In this context, political parties found they had high incentives to compete to mobilize support through promises to control and restrict migration and asylum.

This restrictive policy agenda has conflicted with the continued pro-migration interests of business, human rights and refugee groups and, in some cases, increasingly organized and vocal ethnic minority groups. In addition, it has been constrained by national constitutional provisions and norms on migrant and refugee rights, as well as by emerging EU policy on free movement, immigration and asylum. The new constellation of interests and considerations determining policy is therefore highly complex. It engages a far wider range of actors who feel they have a stake in immigration policies, and who are deeply divided over the desirability of immigration.

MIGRATION AND REFUGEE POLICIES BEFORE 1973

**Immigration as a product of labour needs and post-colonial commitments**

Until the 1970s, migration policy decisions in most European immigrant receiving states were dominated by labour market and demographic considerations. This was most clearly the case in France, West Germany, the Netherlands, Belgium, Austria and Switzerland, all of which recruited additional labour through so-called 'guest worker' schemes in the 1950s, 1960s and early 1970s. Faced with a shortage of workers, these countries were heavily reliant on labour immigration for postwar reconstruction and economic expansion. For a variety of reasons, decisions on how many migrants to admit, and the length and conditions of their stay, tended to be made by governments and their social partners without wider public debate.

This clientelist model was apparent in West Germany between the late 1940s and the mid-1970s. After the Second World War, West Germany had been able to draw on the roughly 10 million ethnic German refugees who had arrived between 1946 and 1949 as a source of labour, and also on substantial numbers of East Germans crossing to the west before 1961. As these flows dried up, Germany began to look to Mediterranean countries as a source of labour migration to underpin its industrial expansion. The government concluded its first bilateral agreement on guest workers with Italy in 1955, an arrangement which regulated questions of recruitment, employment, social conditions for labour migrants and provisions on family reunion.[2] Subsequent agreements were concluded in the 1960s with Spain, Greece, Turkey, Portugal, Tunisia, Morocco and Yugoslavia. The level of migration, and conditions for stay, were agreed upon by the Federal Employment Office in consultation with employers and trade unions.

The lack of parliamentary debate or public scrutiny partly reflected the fact that migration was seen as almost exclusively a matter of economic policy.[3] Decisions on immigration during this period were based on labour needs, and the recruitment, employment and living conditions of immigrants were controlled, at least initially, by the ministry in Bonn. Moreover, it was assumed that a rotation system of labour migrants would ensure that the stay of migrants was temporary, so that they would not establish roots in Germany. What public debate there was on immigration tended to extol the economic wisdom of this form of temporary labour migration. It was argued that guest workers (*Gastarbeiter*) filled gaps in the labour market, particularly in low-skilled industrial work. They paid taxes and welfare contributions, while imposing below-average social costs (largely because their families remained at home, and it was assumed that they would retire in their countries of origin). Most saved money to send home, implying low consumption and helping to dampen inflationary pressures. Further, it was assumed that in the event of rising unemployment in West Germany, guest workers would simply return to their countries of origin. Most sections of the media and all political parties appeared convinced of the case for guest-worker migration.[4]

Although Germany continued to insist right up until the late 1990s that it was not a country of immigration, the guest-worker scheme led to a huge rise in its foreign population, with a net immigration of 12.6 million between 1950 and 1993.[5] Between 1960 and 1973 alone, the foreign element of the workforce rose from 2 per cent to 11 per cent.[6] The level of immigration could not fail to have a significant social as well as economic impact; and, as we shall see, even before the recession of 1973 the issue was gradually becoming more politically contested.

France's postwar migration policy was also characterized by the recruitment of large numbers of foreign workers, a policy which, as in the German case, remained outside the domain of party political debate. This was in large part because of the widespread acceptance of the economic and demographic case for immigration in France. From 1946 onwards there was a broad consensus that immigration was the only means of solving France's drastic shortage of labour. As in Germany, the details of policy were left to the government and its social partners to work out.[7]

In addition to the economic argument, French policy was also influenced by the importance of retaining good relations with former or existing colonies. Most notably, Algeria retained special status as an overseas territory, with legislation of 1947 granting its nationals French citizenship, thereby enabling hundreds of thousands of Algerians to settle in France.[8] Close ties with other Maghreb countries and with former colonies in west Africa also constrained French governments from introducing restrictions on African immigrants until the early 1970s.[9] This was not uncontroversial, and French political elites were concerned about the impact of large-scale immigration from Algeria and other African countries on France's cultural identity. French governments therefore simultaneously attempted to recruit labour from other European countries, concluding a bilateral agreement with Italy in 1947, followed by agreements with Greece, Spain and Portugal.

Belgium recruited labour migrants from Italy, Spain, Greece, Morocco and Turkey in the 1950s and 1960s, to work in almost all sectors of the economy. Migration was planned and organized by the government and Belgian businesses, showing the same pattern of client politics.[10] Belgium received significant numbers of immigrants from its former colony, Congo (Zaire), although the largest groups were Italians and Moroccans. By 1970 it had a total of 700,000 foreign residents.[11] In the 1960s the Netherlands and Austria introduced schemes to import guest workers from southern Europe, Turkey and North Africa. Labour migration to the Netherlands was composed mainly of Turkish and Moroccan immigrants, with flows peaking in 1970–71. The country's colonial ties also drew migrants from Surinam and the Dutch Antilles. Austria's labour migration was composed of predominantly Yugoslav and Turkish guest workers.

The UK experience with migration policy was somewhat different from that of its continental neighbours. The government did introduce limited schemes for recruiting labour in the 1940s, but there was far less recognition of the necessity of foreign labour for economic reconstruction.[12] Instead, the rise in the UK's foreign population over this period can be attributed largely to foreign policy considerations, particularly relations with colonies and New Commonwealth countries.[13] Until the early 1960s, subjects of the British Empire were entitled to British passports under the 1948 British Nationality Act. The first large numbers of immigrants began arriving from the West Indies in 1948, and by spring 1950 there were around 25,000 Caribbean immigrants in the UK.[14] The Labour government of the day was clearly concerned over the question of integrating large numbers of immigrants from the West Indies, and the cabinet debated the possibility of amending the Nationality Act in order to limit migration. However, this step was considered too politically damaging to already sensitive relations with colonies and Commonwealth countries.[15] West Indian immigration was followed by substantial immigration from India and Pakistan in the 1950s and 1960s. By 1961 the number of residents of West Indian origin had risen to 171,800; those of Indian origin numbered 81,400, with 24,900 of Pakistani origin.[16]

From the outset the immigration issue was a subject of popular concern in the UK, mainly revolving around issues of race, welfare costs and integration. One reason for the preoccupation with integration was the fact that, unlike in the case of continental guest-worker models, immigrants were granted full socio-economic, civil and political rights, and it was assumed from fairly early on that they would stay in the UK. As migration movements were not managed in the way they were in continental countries, there were also concerns about an apparently limitless source of potential migrants from (former) colonies.

Attitudes towards New Commonwealth immigrants were not helped by the absence of a strong public defence of the economic case for immigration. Some businesses did argue for increased immigration on economic grounds, but political parties, and even the Trades Union Congress, preferred to stress the political or moral case for admitting immigrants from the West Indies and the Indian subcontinent.[17] Such arguments held little weight with large sections of the British public, many of whom saw immigration as a threat to their cultural identity, jobs and welfare. In response to concerns about race relations and the welfare costs of immigration, as well as to a spate of race riots instigated by anti-immigrant groups from 1958 onwards, the UK introduced a series of laws in the 1960s and in 1971 to limit access to British citizenship and to restrict immigration.[18]

Just as the UK was engaged in tightening up its immigration policy, continental European countries were finding that they were under pressure to broaden theirs. Assumptions about temporary migration or rotation systems proved unrealistic, as many immigrants ended up settling in their host countries, often being joined by their families. At the same time, states found that they had to assume increasing obligations regarding the rights and welfare of long-term residents. One source of this expansion of rights was national constitutional commitments, which were often expansively interpreted by courts. West Germany was a classic example of this pattern; its courts successively broadened the rights of immigrants through a series of decisions in the 1970s and 1980s on deportation, residence permits and family reunion.[19] The extension of social rights to ethnic minority residents undermined the assumption that immigration could simply be treated as a subset of economic policy. The guest workers of the 1950s and 1960s were clearly there to stay, raising a number of issues about multiculturalism, citizenship and identity. Moreover, they and their families were entitled to a range of social and welfare services, implying that the strong fiscal advantages of labour migration might no longer apply. Western Europe's age of innocence in migration policy appeared to be over.

## Responses to refugees in the Cold War era

While migration policies after the Second World War were dominated by economic considerations in most continental immigration countries, refugee policy was far more influenced by international political considerations, especially the Cold War. In the late 1940s, west European states and the United States had agreed to establish a new United Nations agency to deal with refugees, and in 1951 they signed the Geneva Convention on the Status of Refugees. From the outset, the international refugee regime was charged with political symbolism. The 1951 Convention defined refugees as those with 'a well-founded fear of being persecuted for reasons of race, religion, nationality, membership of a particular social group or political opinion'.[20] The definition was based on emerging norms of individual human rights but, as has subsequently been argued, with a bias towards civil and political rights rather than economic, social and cultural ones.[21] It was clearly designed to embrace those fleeing persecution in communist countries, and indeed over the next two decades refugee policy became a powerful symbol of Western liberalism.

At the time the Convention was drafted, there was already some anxiety on the part of west European states that the provisions on refugee protection were too generous. France, the Netherlands, Italy and West Germany all stressed that the Convention should be restricted to dealing with individual refugee arrivals, excluding cases of mass influx.[22] There were concerns that the commitment not to return refugees to places where their 'lives or liberty' would be at risk, the principle of *non-refoulement*, would impose inordinate obligations in cases of large-scale influx.

Despite their reservations, most west European states incorporated these provisions on refugees and asylum into their national legislation. Indeed, many had already codified similar provisions in their constitutions. The 1949 West German Basic Law incorporated a broadly defined right to asylum, offering asylum-seekers access to a range of legal and constitutional rights, including the right to appeal before the constitutional court.[23] It also incorporated provisions on so-called 'Convention' refugee status in subsequent legislation, effectively creating two frameworks for granting refugee status: the Basic Law and the 1951 Geneva Convention. The 1946 French Constitution similarly granted a right to asylum, and the Geneva Convention was subsequently incorporated into French legislation of 1952, which also set out procedures for determining refugee status. In the UK the Convention was referred to in legislation, and although it lacked the more robust constitutional basis enjoyed in France and Germany, it clearly guided British refugee and asylum policy.

The concerns voiced by some states about large-scale influx may have seemed rather exaggerated in the 1950s. To be sure, there was a steady trickle of individual refugees, primarily from the Eastern bloc, as well as sporadic cases of larger flows of refugees following particular political crises. Around 200,000 refugees fled Hungary after the 1956 revolution, and a similar number escaped Czechoslovakia after the Soviet invasion in 1968.[24] But restrictions on emigration from the Soviet bloc for the most part kept the numbers of refugees limited, and the continued demand for labour raised no perceived conflict with the national interests of receiving states in western Europe. Both of these factors, as well as the ideological symbolism of refugee flows from the East, meant that west European states were by and large happy to accept refugees.

However, this system for protecting refugees began to create problems in the 1970s. The 1973 oil crisis and the ensuing recession produced high unemployment, and anxieties about jobs and welfare in west European states triggered demands for a stop to labour migration. In 1973–4 almost all continental European states halted labour migration schemes. As states closed channels for legal migration, many people who would otherwise have entered through guest-worker programmes turned to the remaining routes for entry into industrialized states: family reunion and asylum.

Meanwhile, civil conflict in a number of former colonies created a wave of 'new refugees', from developing countries, many of whom sought asylum in west European states. In the face of rising numbers of applicants for asylum, public concern about the apparent costs of migration began to shift to a focus on the problem of asylum-seekers and the costs of receiving them. For the first time, the liberal provisions codified in international refugee law and incorporated into west European constitutions and legislation began to be seriously questioned.

## THE POLITICIZATION OF MIGRATION AND REFUGEE POLICIES

### The UK: 'swamped' by immigrants and asylum-seekers

If migration and refugee policies had been determined largely by domestic economic concerns and international politics in the postwar era, from the 1970s onwards they became increasingly the subject of domestic political debate. As already noted, the UK was the first to experience significant overt anti-immigrant sentiment and inter-ethnic tensions, with race riots in 1958 and the 1960s bringing the issue to the fore. Yet the main political parties in the UK managed to reach consensus on the broad strokes of policy: the prevailing view was that the restriction of immigration was necessary to avoid fuelling social tensions and to ensure the integration of already resident ethnic minorities.[25] Hence from the 1960s onwards British policy combined a series of restrictive entry laws with efforts to improve what were rather anachronistically termed 'race relations'. For the most part, politicians avoided exploiting the immigration issue, ensuring that race and migration did not become major electoral issues in the 1960s and 1970s. Enoch Powell's anti-immigration stance in the late 1960s, although attracting significant public support, led to his political marginalization in the Conservative Party. It was simply not acceptable to play the 'race card'.

Anti-immigrant discourse became more mainstream in political debate in the late 1970s. Against a background of rising inter-ethnic tensions, in 1978 the new Conservative leader, Margaret Thatcher, made a speech expressing concern about Britain being 'swamped by people with a different culture'.[26] Following their election victory in 1979, the Conservatives introduced a law in 1981 to restrict family reunion and halt the automatic right of citizenship for those born on British soil.

One reason for this more strident rhetoric was growing apprehension about the economic impact of immigration, especially at a time of high unemployment. The Conservative Party was able to tap into popular concerns about the perceived competition for jobs between nationals and foreign workers, as well as the welfare costs of assisting migrants and asylum-seekers. These concerns about protecting jobs and welfare rights were not just a response to the 1970s recession, but almost certainly reflected anxieties about the radical economic restructuring and welfare state reforms of the 1980s.[27] The Conservative Party, which remained in power until 1997, sought to mobilize support by combining a neo-liberal economic agenda with a more protectionist policy *vis-à-vis* foreign policy and immigration. In effect, it was an attempt to mitigate the destabilizing impact of neo-liberal reforms with a nationalist rhetoric which promised to guard citizens against external threats – whether in the form of a robust defence of the UK's interests in the European Community or the Falklands or through protecting Britain from an influx of New Commonwealth immigrants or asylum-seekers.

Arguably, the changing nature of the migration 'problem' made such rhetoric less controversial. In the late 1980s and especially the 1990s the focus of popular media and party political debate shifted from immigration issues to anti-asylum rhetoric. This was in large part a function of rising numbers of asylum-seekers (even though the numbers seeking asylum in the UK remained relatively low until 1990). It also reflected the relatively lower political risk of targeting this group. Hostility towards asylum-seekers was usually justified on grounds of problems of abuse of welfare and asylum systems rather than based on arguments about race or ethnic relations. This rhetoric was, at least in theory, compatible with an endorsement of multicultural Britain and the goal of further integrating ethnic minority groups. Both main political parties in the UK played on this distinction between already resident ethnic minority groups and burdensome newcomers who were portrayed as abusing the asylum system. Thus despite differences in proposed policy responses, the Labour and Conservative parties gradually forged a new policy consensus, which was essentially a variant of the compromise that had emerged in the 1960s: restrictive entry, this time targeted at asylum-seekers and illegal immigrants, combined with policies to promote the integration of resident ethnic groups.[28]

In addition to these domestic dynamics, a number of international political developments contributed to the politicization of refugee and migration policy in the UK. The declining importance of its relations with former colonies undoubtedly made it less cautious about the impact of restrictive migration policies on foreign relations. By the 1980s, the thaw in East–West relations also reduced the political significance of asylum policies. The salience of foreign policy considerations in shaping refugee policy was overshadowed by concerns about the domestic social and economic impact of receiving large numbers of asylum-seekers.

## Germany: facing up to permanent immigration and asylum-seekers

The demise of Cold War politics and changing domestic socio-economic conditions also profoundly influenced West German migration and asylum politics in the 1980s. There had been some public hostility to immigrants in 1966–7, at the time of the country's first postwar economic downturn.[29] With the onset of recession in 1973 the economic case for migration was seriously questioned, and the government stopped recruiting guest workers in 1974. Ostensibly, this measure was a direct response to the 'oil shock' and rising unemployment in West Germany. But it must also be understood in the context of concern about the rising social and welfare costs of immigration.[30] In particular, there was growing anxiety about the question of integrating Turkish guest workers, many of whom were effectively becoming permanent residents. On this interpretation, the oil crisis may have provided a justification for making a sensitive policy decision, rather than being the main rationale prompting it.

Despite restrictions on guest-worker entry, the number of Turkish residents in Germany rose in the 1970s, largely because of family reunion, and by 1981 they were the largest minority group, standing at 1.4 million.[31] The issue of continued immigration became a major subject of party political debate in the early 1980s. With the recruitment ban already in place, the debate began to revolve around questions of family reunion and the return of guest workers. The new chancellor, Helmut Kohl, was keen to draw attention to the problem, in what was to become a pattern of political mobilization on immigration issues. Shortly after he took office in 1982, Kohl announced that Germany's policy on foreigners was one of the four most urgent issues facing the government, and stated his goal of reducing the foreign population by one million.[32] However, the attempt by Kohl's centre-right coalition (Christlich Demokratische Union–Christlich Soziale Union–Freie Demokratische Partei (CDU–CSU–FDP)) in 1983–4 to encourage the return of guest workers to their country of origin had a limited impact. Around 300,000 immigrants returned as a result of the *Rückkehrgesetz* (Return Law), but this figure was no higher than the number of those who had returned spontaneously in previous years – the number of returnees had been over 365,000 per year since 1973.[33] Meanwhile, the state's leverage over family reunion was restricted by a constitutional court ruling of 1987. Compared to Kohl's tougher rhetoric in the early 1980s, the subsequent Foreigners Law of 1990 was surprisingly moderate, essentially consolidating existing rules on reunion and residence.[34]

By the late 1970s, anti-immigrant sentiment in West Germany had also begun to focus on the asylum question. West Germany experienced a far higher increase than any other European country in the number of asylum applications from the 1970s onwards. At the same time, the composition of those seeking asylum was changing, with an increasing proportion arriving from developing countries. The spontaneous arrival of asylum-seekers from Asia and the Far East contrasted with the selected and controlled arrival of mainly Mediterranean nationals through guest-worker schemes. These 'new refugees' were for the most part not products of communist persecution, and thus had a quite different profile from the refugees envisaged by West Germany's generous Cold War-era asylum system. As early as 1972–3 there were discussions about how to tackle asylum *Mißbrauch*, or 'abuse',[35] and by the late 1970s the CDU- and CSU-dominated federal states were increasingly criticizing the Sozial Demokratische Partei (SPD)–FDP central government for its failure to control the asylum problem.[36] As in the UK, political parties began to tap into popular fears about the state's inability or unwillingness to protect the socio-economic privileges of members from unwanted newcomers.

Legislation in 1981 had already introduced a number of measures designed to deter asylum-seekers and lower the costs of the asylum system.

However, the exponential rise in asylum-seekers over the next decade, coupled with the large-scale immigration of ethnic Germans from central and eastern Europe after 1989, generated what was widely characterized as an immigration crisis in Germany. Between 1989 and 1992 Germany had to absorb three million immigrants, and it received over a quarter of a million displaced persons from the conflict in the former Yugoslavia. The level of racist attacks rose alarmingly in the early 1990s. Many of these occurred in the new eastern *Länder*, which were undergoing radical socio-economic and political upheaval and had little experience of receiving immigrants. Responding to the perceived crisis, the government introduced legislation in 1993 which revised the Basic Law so as to limit access to asylum. Subsequent legislation in 1997 and 1998 further restricted access to the asylum system and narrowed the criteria for recognizing refugees, and it reduced the standards of social assistance for asylum-seekers. Germany also concluded a series of bilateral agreements with central and east European countries committing the latter to readmit migrants and asylum-seekers who had illegally crossed their borders into Germany.

As in the UK, then, from the 1970s onwards immigrants and asylum-seekers were seen as a cause of socio-economic insecurity and also as a threat to notions of shared cultural identity. Centre-right parties in Germany were, if anything, more willing than their British counterparts to exploit these fears in the 1980s. One reason for this was the rise of the far-right Republikaner Party, which kept migration issues on the agenda and probably encouraged the CDU and CSU to incorporate anti-migration policies into their programmes.

These parties also drew on a tradition of defining citizenship in terms of the German *Volk,* which justified an ethnicity-based conception of citizenship. Although German policies were influenced and constrained by a strong constitutional commitment to human rights, a number of centre-right politicians continued to draw on this ethnic notion of citizenship in the 1980s and 1990s in order to justify the exclusion of immigrants. It was a conception which had popular resonance at a time of socio-economic insecurity and (after 1989) radical political change. And until 1990, it was one that served to legitimize West Germany's continued claims to reunification with the east and its support for ethnic Germans in central and eastern Europe.[37]

## France: challenges to identity and control

The far right played a much greater role in the politicization of migration issues in France, with the issue exploding onto the political scene in the early 1980s. Questions of integration and the socio-economic impact of immigration had already come to the fore in the 1970s. Between 1977 and 1981 the government had attempted to encourage the return of immigrants to their home country and to introduce a series of measures to restrict entry and facilitate expulsions. In the early 1980s the new Parti Socialiste (PS) government adopted a policy of restricting new immigration while improving the conditions of long-term residents. Policy also focused on the rising problem of irregular migration, and in 1981–2 the government introduced an amnesty to regularize the situation of those illegally resident in France. However, this relatively liberal approach was fiercely challenged by the far-right Front National (FN), which was successfully mobilizing support on an anti-immigrant platform. The FN had a substantial impact on the debate on immigration, helping to shift the focus from a predominantly economic issue to a perceived socio-economic threat.[38] The party made considerable electoral gains in 1983 and 1984, winning control of Dreux in municipal elections in 1984 and gaining 11 per cent of the national vote in the European elections that year.

The FN's success forced mainstream parties to reassess their immigration policies, with the PS retreating from its liberal agenda and the right wing incorporating many elements of the far right's agenda. The 1986 Gaullist–Union pour la Démocratie Française (UDF) administration pursued a tough, control-based approach and attempted to tighten France's rules on citizenship. Interior Minister Charles Pasqua's proposals for reform were opposed by a range of non-governmenal organizations (NGOs), church organizations and political parties. A special Commission des Sages, established to assess the notion of French citizenship, also rejected many of the proposals, instead reaffirming the importance of the relatively expansive French republican model of citizenship. Attempts to radically tighten asylum laws were frustrated too by widespread public protests.[39] This opposition limited the margin for manoeuvre of the Gaullist–UDF government and created space for the FN to continue to mobilize support for more draconian measures. The FN continued to show strong electoral support throughout the 1980s and 1990s.

Proposals to reform France's still generous asylum system did not emerge until the 1990s. Before then, the focus of discussion had been on illegal migration, integration and citizenship. The relatively generous asylum rules had so far gone untouched. In 1991, a ministerial circular denied asylum-seekers access to the labour market. Further changes were proposed in 1993, when Pasqua, reappointed as interior minister, put forward a package of reforms to restrict many of the rights of immigrants and asylum-seekers. The so-called second Pasqua law included provisions to restrict asylum-seekers' right of appeal against a negative decision. The proposals were again strongly contested by human rights groups, and the constitutional court rejected the provisions on asylum-seekers on the grounds that they contravened the 1946 constitution.[40] In response, Pasqua proposed an amendment of the French constitutional provisions on asylum. His central justification was that such a reform was necessary in order to bring French law in line with emerging EU policies. Subsequent legislation in 1996 under the Interior Minister Jean-Louis Debré further tightened laws on the rights of foreigners and introduced measures to restrict illegal migration.

In the late 1990s, however, policy under the PS government led by Lionel Jospin returned to the more liberal and republican tradition, restoring elements of previous provisions on naturalization. Apart from the continued campaigning of the FN on migration issues, calls for more restrictive measures appeared to have died down by the end of the 1990s; migration and asylum were no longer a central topic of party political debate. This may be changing now, with the increasing focus on issues of law and order in French politics, which is often linked to questions of illegal migration and criminality among the immigrant population. Such concerns certainly contributed to the FN's spectacular result in the first round of the April 2002 presidential elections.

## Italy: political crisis, the far right and illegal immigration

By the 1980s the traditional migrant-sending countries of southern Europe – Italy, Spain, Greece and Portugal – were becoming receiving countries. Italy represents an interesting example of how rapidly immigration issues can rise to the top of the political agenda. Emigration from Italy was declining in the early 1970s, and in 1973 the level of return migration of Italians exceeded emigration for the first time.[41] Italy also started receiving substantial numbers of immigrants from Africa and Asia in the 1970s, in large part because of restricted opportunities for immigration to other west European countries.[42] By 1977 there were an estimated 300,000–400,000 immigrants in Italy, a number which had risen to almost 900,000 by 1991.[43] A combination of restrictive legislation on immigrants, high demand for irregular labour in many sectors and lax application of migration controls meant that most migrants were irregular and worked in the informal sector. This situation continued until the mid-1980s, with public opinion remaining largely indifferent to the issue of immigration and business keen to maintain its source of cheap labour.

It was only in 1985 that migration came to the fore as a policy issue. The Socialist Prime Minister Bettino Craxi publicly linked the problem of terrorism to uncontrolled immigration, triggering a public debate on border controls and illegal immigration.[44] A law of 1986 introduced improved rights for foreign workers, penalties for illegal entry and employment and an amnesty for irregular migrants. The law had limited success: there were far fewer regularizations than expected and a number of gaps in the provisions on immigration. However, it did temporarily allay concerns about irregular migration and illegal employment.

Italian politics continued to be relatively inactive in the area of migration control until the 1990s. One explanation for this was a generally tolerant public attitude towards irregular migration and employment. The residence and employment of immigrants was by and large not seen as threatening the jobs of nationals or imposing welfare costs (see Chapter 3). Moreover, the two main parties of government, as well as the social partners (trade unions and employer groups), NGOs and the Catholic Church were all keen to promote a moderate, non-racist stance. Even the neo-fascist Movimento Sociale Italiano (MSI) was cautious about pursuing an overtly anti-immigration stance, preferring to stick with its traditional anti-communist agenda.

This situation changed from the late 1980s onwards, with growing public concerns about the social situation of illegal immigrants, many of whom were without accommodation or social assistance and lived in self-constructed camps on the edges of Italian cities. Italy was also under much pressure from other European Community states to control irregular migration flows. The Martelli Law of 1990 attempted to reassure other European countries of Italy's commitment to tackling the problem, introducing a number of provisions on migration control. It also included measures on labour immigration and asylum-seekers' rights and introduced a second amnesty for irregular migrants, this time with more take-up than in the case of the 1986 programme. The law was in many ways inadequate, however, as it failed to seriously address the problems of immigrant integration or to manage the problem of illegal influx and irregular labour.

Two main developments contributed to the rapid politicization of migration in the early 1990s. First was the rising problem of illegal migration into Italy, a phenomenon caused in part by political crises in the former Yugoslavia and Albania and the expansion of people-smuggling networks using Mediterranean sea routes. Increasingly restrictive migration and asylum legislation in other EU states also made Italy a more attractive destination for many illegal migrants. The second development was the collapse of support for the traditional mainstream parties in 1992–3, which led to a surge in support for the anti-immigrant far right. As Chapter 3 shows, the Polo delle Libertà coalition parties (subsequently Casa delle Libertà), including Slivio Berlusconi's Forza Italia, the Alleanza Nazionale (formerly MSI) and the Lega Nord, owed much of their electoral success to their tough stance on the growing problem of illegal migration. They were able to exploit what has been coined the Italian 'invasion syndrome', fears of uncontrolled migration into Italy.[45] Right-wing populist parties benefited from the political opportunities created by the failure of previous moderate governments to manage migration, as well as from the ideological gap created by the new crisis of the postwar political system. Thus from being a country of emigration Italy moved to being a net recipient of migration in the late 1970s, and by the early 1990s the question had become one of the most urgent policy issues of the day.

## THE LIMITS TO RESTRICTION

While most west European states were keen to restrict migration in the 1980s and 1990s, they also encountered a range of obstacles to pursuing traditional domestic control measures. Various interests and constraints limited the effectiveness of border and internal control measures and of attempts to reduce the welfare and rights of immigrants and asylum-seekers.

### Domestic constraints

One limitation stemmed from the various lobby and interest groups campaigning against restrictive measures. A range of church, migrant, refugee and human rights groups such as the United Nations High Commission for Refugees, Amnesty International and national NGOs were critical of practices that adversely affected refugees and immigrants. Increasingly, trade union movements too began to incorporate the interests of migrant workers, although some have been ambivalent on the question of admitting more immigrants. More significantly, business continued to be strongly in favour of more liberal rules on admitting migrants. In many sectors, such as agriculture, manufacturing, catering and tourism, employers were still dependent on a supply of cheap, flexible labour to do jobs that nationals were unwilling to take on. When this demand could no longer be met by official guest-worker schemes, many firms relied on the illegal employment of irregular immigrants. Indeed, the increase in irregular migration in the 1980s was to a large extent a function of this continued demand for labour in many west European states.

Governments were clearly sensitive to pressure from business, and in many cases continued to offer legal possibilities for recruiting temporary or seasonal labour to various sectors throughout the 1980s and 1990s. Thus France kept open possibilities for temporary and seasonal work, allowing thousands of seasonal workers from Morocco, Tunisia, Yugoslavia and Poland to work for periods of six months. In the 1990s, Germany admitted legal seasonal workers from Poland and other central European states, with over 200,000 staying for periods of three months.[46] Rules also remained open to admit various categories of skilled workers, including senior staff of multinational companies, successful entrepreneurs, academics and artists.

A second limitation on restrictive policies was the influence of constitutional and human rights commitments. We saw in the case of West Germany how a number of court rulings forced the state to introduce more generous provisions on family reunion, deportation and residence permits. The right to asylum set out in Article 16 of the Basic Law meanwhile acted as a considerable constraint on reforms to asylum policy until it was finally amended in 1993. French governments were similarly constrained by constitutional commitments, as well as by opposition from human rights and anti-racist groups. On several occasions right-wing governments were frustrated in their attempts to introduce more restrictive policies on asylum law, naturalization and the rights of immigrants.[47] In the UK, which has no codified constitution and, until recently, had no human rights act, European Court of Human Rights decisions were a major constraint on the treatment of asylum-seekers. Thus, for example, the Court ruled against the detention of a number of applicants and against the deportation of certain rejected asylum-seekers. The British High Court also had considerable influence upon ensuring a wide interpretation of the definition of 'refugee', for instance in the case of gender-based persecution, and it ruled against the return of applicants to France and Germany because of these countries' overly narrow interpretation of the Geneva Convention.[48]

Another constraint on introducing more draconian migration control measures was related to their impact on inter-ethnic relations. European states with sizeable resident ethnic minority groups have realized that the introduction of policies that ratchet down the rights and welfare standards of asylum-seekers or stigmatize illegal immigrants can have negative repercussions for inter-ethnic relations. Such measures can imply racial discrimination against particular groups in the distribution of rights and welfare benefits, and can touch on sensitive issues about the membership and integration of current minority residents. Such concerns have been consistently present in the British debate on migration policy, which has tended to be especially sensitive to problems of racial discrimination and inter-ethnic relations. They have also surfaced more recently in the context of UK policy on asylum-seekers, with a number of groups criticizing measures to decrease benefits and introduce vouchers for asylum-seekers as jeopardizing race relations.[49]

These considerations have gained weight as the political and civil rights of long-term residents have been expanded. Where ethnic minorities have been granted voting rights, European political parties have had to show more sensitivity to the concerns of resident minorities. This has clearly had an impact on integration policies and has contributed to a less ethnocentric or racially discriminatory discourse on immigration questions.

A fourth limitation on introducing more stringent control measures is concern about their impact on civil rights in general. States such as the United Kingdom with a tradition of minimalist state intervention have found it difficult to control the residence and movement of immigrants.[50] Recent debates about the possible introduction of identity cards in the UK as an anti-terrorist measure illustrate the conflict between internal controls and civil liberties. Most continental countries have a stronger tradition of state monitoring of the residence and movement of citizens, making certain internal checks on immigrants relatively less controversial. But attempts to exert greater control over non-nationals have also run up against resistance on civil rights grounds in France, as in the case of the proposals in 1996 that citizens must notify local authorities whenever they receive non-EU visitors.[51]

## International cooperation: constraint and opportunity

National capacities to control immigration have also been eroded by international and especially European developments. At the European Union level, the creation of a single market permitting the free movement of workers has removed the prerogative of states to restrict the entry, residence and employment of citizens of EU or European Economic Area (EEA) states. Although relocation of EEA nationals between states remains relatively limited, the prospect of free movement for new EU member states in central and eastern Europe has been an issue of major political concern for a number of current member states.[52] For members of the Schengen Group,[53] the abolition of internal border checks has removed an important instrument of migration control. In one sense, these constraints on sovereignty over migration policy were self-imposed, and reflect the priority of liberalizing the movement of factors of production between states. Yet as a number of observers have pointed out, they also reveal a deep-seated tension between the logic of economic liberalization and the more protectionist political discourse on migration in most European states.[54]

The abolition of barriers to movement between EU and Schengen states has prompted a number of 'flanking' measures to compensate for this loss of national control of migration. EU cooperation on immigration and asylum issues, which emerged in the second half of the 1980s, was largely a response to this need. These flanking measures have included cooperation to strengthen the external borders of the EU and to limit irregular movement between EU states, to compensate for weaker or non-existent internal controls. The Schengen Agreement contains extensive provisions on external border controls, and in 1990 two further conventions concerned with controlling irregular movement were adopted: the Dublin Convention determining the state responsible for examining asylum applications lodged in one member state, designed in effect to limit what was known as 'country shopping' by asylum-seekers moving between EU states; and the Convention on the Crossing of External Borders, designed to strengthen control of EU external borders.[55]

Cooperation on immigration and asylum issues was formalized in the 1992 Maastricht Treaty and extended by the 1997 Treaty of Amsterdam. Cooperation now covers the harmonization of national provisions on the reception of asylum-seekers, the processing and recognition of asylum applications, temporary protection, the status and treatment of long-term residents and policies on entry, including visas, carrier sanctions as well as closer cooperation to combat illegal migration and trafficking (see Chapter 5). European integration in this area has therefore extended beyond being just a means of compensating for the removal of national sovereignty over entry. In many ways, it has created opportunities for new forms of restriction or control that were not possible at the domestic level. But EU integration also continues to represent a constraint on nation-states in other ways. The problem of increased flows between EU states prompted by the Single European Act (SEA) and the Schengen Agreement has not fully been compensated for through cooperation on immigration and asylum. The need to approximate legislation has also put pressure on some states to liberalize provisions on naturalization, the treatment of long-term residents and asylum law.

A second international response to limited capacity to control migration has been to develop so-called 'alternatives' to asylum. Since the early 1990s west European states have shown considerable interest in promoting what have been termed 'new solutions' to refugee problems, which aim to eliminate or reduce the need for people to seek asylum in Europe. Thus various proposals have been mooted about promoting refugee 'reception in the region', through assessing asylum claims in offices abroad, funding refugee camps in countries of asylum in the region, or reinforcing human rights monitoring in places of origin.[56] Ideas about preventing migration and refugee flows through addressing the causes of movement have also been popular. There have been several EU statements on the need to develop such preventive approaches; indeed in 1999 the EU committed itself to integrating these goals into its external policy.[57] Other proposed 'alternatives' to asylum have included reinforcing protection for internally displaced people and supporting the early repatriation of refugees following ethnic conflict. The emergence of so-called 'temporary protection' for people fleeing civil conflict was likewise designed to relieve west European states of the perceived burden of granting asylum to large numbers of refugees.

Yet none of these approaches – classic domestic migration restriction, regional cooperation and alternatives to asylum – has had resounding success in limiting flows. National measures to restrict access to asylum systems appear to have had some impact on applications in particular states, but overall numbers of asylum-seekers in the EU have not decreased, suggesting that tightening provisions in one country simply leads to increased numbers in other EU states. EU attempts to promote a balance of efforts through harmonizing legislation and providing financial assistance for states receiving higher numbers of asylum-seekers and refugees may help to achieve a more proportionate distribution of costs, but they do not appear to limit the overall numbers of those seeking asylum in EU states.

Meanwhile, the restriction of possibilities for legal entry into EU states has, as already noted, led to burgeoning illegal migration and the use of migrant-traffickers to gain access to Europe. As national and EU cooperation to combat the trafficking and smuggling of migrants has intensified, traffickers and smugglers have developed transnational networks and started using increasingly sophisticated equipment. Human trafficking is now a highly lucrative business netting over $7 billion per year, and appears to be an expanding area for networks already involved in drugs- and weapons-trafficking.[58] Efforts at European cooperation have so far been unable to make significant headway in tackling the problem. Measures to strengthen external borders do not appear to have limited the numbers of migrants attempting to cross the Adriatic or the Strait of Gibraltar into southern EU countries, while attempts to strengthen the eastern borders of potential new member states have led to substantial problems in relations with neighbouring states to the east, as has been widely documented.[59] West European migration policies have therefore been unable to deter or prevent the movement of people trying to find protection or a better standard of life.

CONCLUSION

The quest to control migration and refugee flows that began in most countries in 1973–4 has in many senses proved elusive. Although governments have been keen to demonstrate their capacity to limit the number and costs of migrants and refugees, various domestic and international factors have combined to frustrate their attempts. Some of these constraints can be attributed to lack of planning or inefficient administrative procedures, as has often been the case for asylum systems. Others are tensions that appear to be endemic in the norms, goals and structures of liberal democratic states. Migration restriction may be popular with electorates, but it conflicts with business interests and with the goal of economic liberalization, concerns which are dear to most centrist political parties and exert a huge impact on all governments. Moreover, attempts to introduce tougher controls on asylum-seekers, refugees and illegal migrants run up against human and civil rights norms in liberal democratic states.

European states are still struggling to find the right balance between the competing claims of the politics of restriction and the various pressures to remain open. As shown in Chapter 2, these conflicts are being intensified by pressures to recruit more labour migrants. Yet unlike in the postwar era of labour migration, governments and their social partners no longer have autonomy over migration policies. The politicization of migration and asylum over the past three decades has radically changed the configuration of interests influencing policy. There appears to be no going back to the cosy clientelism of the 1950s and 1960s. Any moves towards a liberalization of asylum or migration rules will need to be fought out in the public arena.

# 2

## *New policies on labour migration*

In February 2000, the German government announced the introduction of a Green Card scheme for up to 20,000 highly skilled workers. This appeared to represent a major shift from the earlier rhetoric of Germany as 'not a country of immigration' and a departure from the restrictionist migration policies of the 1980s and 1990s. Nor was Germany alone in expanding provisions for legal immigration. The UK, which had also pursued stringent controls on immigration since the late 1960s, had already begun to consider ways of loosening its provisions in 1998.

It is important not to exaggerate how far this represented a substantive shift in policy. Even during the restrictionist era of the 1980s and 1990s most west European states had kept open some limited channels for legal migration, through temporary or seasonal worker schemes or the recruitment of high-skilled migrants. Moreover, many had been ambivalent about enforcing measures to control irregular labour migration, which benefited many industries.[1]

But despite these lines of continuity and the fairly limited nature of the policy reforms, the reforms, and the way in which they were justified, were significant in two senses. First, underlying these apparently modest changes was a recognition of the inadequacy of previous policies in responding to a range of new pressures. Although governments and business may always have recognized the case for (at least limited) labour migration, a number of international economic trends and changing labour market structures and demographic patterns lent the arguments far greater urgency than before. The often confusing array of provisions for legal immigration were recognized as inadequate in responding to these new pressures. Secondly, the expansion, however limited, of legal migration channels was of symbolic political importance: after the restrictionist rhetoric of the 1990s, a number of European and particularly centre-left governments appeared once again to be willing to make the case for additional migration.

This chapter examines the factors that have generated this change of approach, looking at the arguments and interests supporting more liberal migration policies. It discusses four main sets of arguments which appear to have strengthened the case for the new policies: the impact of globalization, gaps in labour supply, concerns about ageing populations and the possibility that they may help to control irregular migrant labour. Many of these pressures need to be understood in the context of economic globalization, which has influenced the nature and scale of labour demand and supply and, more generally, has placed pressure on governments to loosen a number of rules on labour mobility. Others relate to the changing demographic structure of European societies, or what are essentially domestic problems of labour supply. The arguments for liberalizing migration rules have powerful backing from business, as well as from the public service sector in some countries. They are also supported by economists and many liberal, centre and centre-left parties committed to economic liberalization. The second part of the chapter addresses how these arguments and interests have influenced migration policies.

In any case, support from elites does not guarantee that such policies are politically acceptable or sustainable within west European states. The concluding part of the chapter briefly examines how public anxiety about the socio-economic impact of migration, as well as continued party political mobilization of anti-immigrant sentiment, could block the emergence of a more liberal agenda in many European countries − themes that will be explored in more depth in subsequent chapters.

THE CASE FOR ECONOMIC MIGRATION

## Globalization and the movement of labour

Much attention has been paid in recent years to the impact of globalization on labour migration.[2] It has been argued that globalization, understood here as the liberalization of trade and the revolution in communications, has both generated displacement and limited the capacity of states to control the influx of migration. Trade liberalization has exerted immense pressure on developing economies, with economic restructuring and increased foreign direct investment (FDI) disrupting traditional work structures and encouraging internal and international migration.[3] Meanwhile, the revolution in communications has exposed millions to Western culture and raised often idealized expectations about opportunities in the West.[4] In addition to these 'push' factors, there is also an important 'pull' factor in industrialized states, as a result of structural demand for cheap, low-skilled labour.[5] As manufacturing companies have been forced to become more flexible and competitive, many have found themselves becoming increasingly dependent on the supply of low-cost, flexible labour, often employed on an irregular basis.[6] One example of this is the phenomenon of 'sweatshops' employing irregular migrants on below legal wages, which have become more widespread in western Europe over the past two decades.

Globalization has also increased demand for high-skilled labour. The revolution in technology and communications means that productivity and competitiveness have become more dependent than ever on having the right knowledge and information.[7] In many sectors, skilled and specialized human capital is now the most valuable factor of production, creating what has been termed a 'knowledge-based economy'. In this economy, firms need to ensure a supply of high-skilled labour, in particular in the information and communications technology (ICT) sector. ICT has also become more important in other sectors such as manufacturing, which is increasingly dependent on these services for greater efficiency and competitiveness.[8] The burgeoning importance of this sector, which in 2000 accounted for around 1.2 million jobs in western Europe, has been a major factor influencing government policies to attract additional ICT workers.[9] The revolution in technology and communications also contributed to the huge expansion of capital markets, worth around $360 trillion, around 12 times the size of global GDP, by 2000.[10] This has generated the expansion of the financial services industry, particularly in financial centres such as London and Frankfurt, again drawing high-, semi- and low-skilled workers from around the world to what have been called 'global centres'.[11]

A second series of pressures linked to globalization is the 'spillover' from trade liberalization, which has prompted states to loosen migration rules in a number of areas. One form this has taken is the liberalization of rules on the mobility of service providers. Service suppliers in many cases need to move with their products, making their mobility an important corollary to the liberalization of the movement of services.[12] Thus the liberalization of trade in services has led to the adoption of new transnational rules on the mobility of service providers under the General Agreement on Trade in Services (GATS), rules which are set to be extended after the current round of negotiations.[13]

Another form of spillover effect is linked to the liberalization of trade and capital movements, which has generated a huge rise in FDI. Multinational corporations (MNCs) dominate FDI, which now accounts for some 70 per cent of world trade and 80 per cent of international investment.[14] It was pointed out above that investment in developing countries by MNCs can generate new patterns of migration, disrupting local labour structures and encouraging emigration. In this sense, foreign direct investment can act as a 'push' factor, creating migration pressures in developing countries. But the importance of attracting investment from MNCs has also pressured the governments of highly industrialized states to open up rules on labour mobility, as MNCs are able to relocate to wherever conditions are the most favourable. This provides a strong incentive for governments to ensure flexible conditions for the movement of their employees, high-skilled managers, executives and service providers, and also to provide 'turnkey' projects, which allow companies to import their own skilled and unskilled labour to carry out particular projects.[15]

Finally, trade liberalization is also encouraging the emergence of regional trade blocs incorporating provisions on the free movement of labour. The European Single Market project is the most evolved example of this type of regional system. In 1986, European Community member states committed themselves to the free movement of workers between them, as part of their objective of removing all physical, technical and fiscal barriers to trade.[16] The abolition of these intra-EC barriers was seen as an important means of enhancing the EC's competitiveness in the global economy. The removal of barriers to free movement was extended to a number of non-EC members in the European Economic Area, including Sweden, Finland and Austria (which have subsequently become EU member states) and Norway (which is still outside the EU). Most EU states have also committed themselves to the Schengen Agreement eliminating border controls between EU states, seen as a corollary of the Single Market project.

Thus globalization has influenced governments to liberalize migration rules in a number of senses. It has changed the structure of production, resulting in a greater demand for both low- and high-skilled labour. Moreover, the liberalization of trade has put pressure on states to loosen restrictions on the movement of service providers and the employees of MNCs, as well as influencing the emergence of regional free movement regimes.

These factors provide at least a partial explanation of recent moves to liberalize migration policies, especially in the fields of services and managerial, executive and technical personnel. They help to explain the continued demand for cheap, flexible labour. However, they do not account for all types of demand: much of the recent discussion has focused on gaps in specific sectors of domestic labour markets which are not obviously linked to globalization. Indeed, it is these domestic arguments about short- to medium-term labour requirements in specific sectors that have tended to dominate the debate on labour migration in west European states.

## Gaps in domestic labour supply

Although globalization may have rendered the case for liberalizing migration rules more pressing, the microeconomic case for labour migration is far from new. There is a substantial body of research suggesting that migration of labour, both skilled and unskilled, is on balance economically beneficial to receiving countries.[17] Public concerns about the displacement of native workers by immigrant labour appear to have little foundation. Immigrants tend to fill gaps in the labour supply, taking jobs that native workers are unable or unwilling to do. In addition, they can act as a cushion against fluctuations in demand, for example in seasonal work such as agriculture or tourism. The displacement of indigenous workers is likely to occur only under specific conditions: where there is high unemployment, where foreign workers are perfectly substitutable for native ones, and where they are willing and able to undercut the costs of native workers.[18] Thus competition for jobs between natives and foreign labour can be a problem in economies with a surplus of labour in particular sectors, inflexible wage structures and a supply of workers with similar skills willing to work for lower wages on an irregular basis. However, it is not likely to be a problem in countries with flexible labour markets, with low unemployment or with strict controls limiting the possibilities for illegal employment. Nor will it be problematic where migrants have skills or job preferences complementary to those of nationals.[19]

The potential economic benefits of skilled immigrant labour are even greater. Skilled migrants can generate new jobs – the Federal Union of German Industry has estimated that each skilled labour migrant creates on average 2.5 new jobs.[20] Hence the notion that there is a finite number of jobs to go around and that migration represents a source of competition to native workers has been, as a recent British Home Office report argues, 'thoroughly discredited'.[21] Instead, an injection of human capital can expand productivity and create new employment. This argument has gained weight with the increased emphasis on the 'knowledge-based economy' referred to in the previous section.

The labour demand argument for increased migration has recently been given additional force by concerns about a number of gaps in labour supply in specific sectors. The first of these is information and communications technology. The exponential rise in the importance of the service sector in developed countries has created substantial skills gaps, leading businesses to push for more liberal rules on admitting foreign specialists. As noted above, much of this demand can be linked to the wider revolution in information and communications. But there are important shortages in other sectors. The UK, Germany and the Netherlands have all experienced serious labour supply gaps in health care services, a shortfall that is set to grow as the proportion of old people in European societies increases. The UK has also had problems in meeting demand in education, with an estimated 10,000 extra teachers needed for England and Wales and gaps in many areas of higher education. These shortages have more to do with inadequate financial renumeration or lack of social prestige in public-sector jobs than with the pressures of globalization.

Not all commentators agree that immigration is the best way of filling these gaps. A number of specialists have argued that although migration may be a relatively efficient way of meeting immediate needs, a long-term solution will require developing measures to ensure a better match between the indigenous labour supply and vacant jobs.[22] Above all, this implies training and retraining of those currently out of work, more efficient recruitment methods and better retention of employees in the public services.[23] Migration may, therefore, be just one of several strategies for meeting labour demand, and possibly not the most effective or sustainable response in the longer term. Nonetheless, for those currently facing supply problems, particularly businesses and public services, the case for migration is far more appealing, as it provides employers with more immediate access to a wider pool of potential labour.

## The demographic argument

The third main argument marshalled in support of more liberal migration policies since the late 1990s has been concern about ageing populations. Fertility rates in west European countries have been declining since the 1960s, while average life expectancy rose from 66 in 1960 to 77 in the late 1990s.[24] Meanwhile, average retirement ages are getting lower, with less than half of the population aged between 55 and 65 in OECD countries in employment.[25] Taken together, these factors are likely to generate a rise in the average age of the population and a decline in the proportion of the population in employment, and thus a rise in the ratio of those dependent on state support to those economically active. Eurostat has estimated that by 2025 the over-65 age group in EU states will constitute 22.4 per cent of the population, in comparison to 15.4 per cent in 1995.[26] A number of studies have argued that the higher old-age dependency ratio will have drastic implications for both productivity and public spending. The decline in the employed population will create a major shortage of labour in all sectors, and a decrease in revenue from taxation. It will also necessitate far greater public expenditure on pensions, health and long-term care. It has been estimated that total public spending could rise by an average of around seven per cent per year between 2000 and 2050.[27]

Some research has suggested that immigration could offset these effects, filling labour gaps and helping to meet public spending costs. A widely cited

UN study argues that the EU would need an intake of almost 674 million immigrants between 2000 and 2050 in order to retain current dependency ratios.[28] Of this aggregate EU figure, the UK would require over one million per year, France 1.8 million, Germany 3.6 million and Italy 2.3 million. Other research has qualified these findings, suggesting that immigration is not a panacea for the problem of ageing populations. Although recruiting young migrant workers may temporarily meet the demand for labour, once they are integrated migrants tend to adopt similar fertility patterns to those of nationals. Thus an increase in immigration will at best delay the process of ageing populations by a few generations: it is not a long-term solution. Moreover, proposals for replacement migration assume public acceptance of a radical increase in the intake of migrants – an assumption which is, to say the least, highly questionable.

Most policy researchers and officials have therefore been more circumspect about advocating migration as a solution to the problem of ageing populations. The European Commission and the OECD have both proposed that limited additional migration be treated as just one part of a wider strategy to address the problem. Other measures would include reforming pension systems and diversifying the sources of retirement income, encouraging older people to stay longer in work, and introducing measures to encourage higher birth rates.[29] Meanwhile, more optimistic commentators have suggested that the predicted contraction of the working-age population could be wholly offset by rising rates of participation in the labour market, for example among the current unemployed, single parents, mothers, and those over 50.[30] It remains questionable, though, whether such reforms could fully meet future labour demand.

## Legal routes as a mechanism of migration control

A fourth prominent argument for more liberal policies is based on the assumption that expanded legal possibilities for labour migration will diminish the level of illegal migration. This argument recognizes that there is a demand for low-skilled immigrant labour in west European states which acts as a 'pull' factor for potential migrants. Where there are no, or only limited, possibilities for filling low-skill vacancies through legal routes, people arrive illegally instead, many using trafficking or smuggling networks, and reside and work clandestinely in EU states. The expansion of legal routes, according to this argument, would reduce the level of illegal entry and labour.

The problems of illegal migration and illegal labour have become a growing headache for west European governments since the 1980s. Of particular concern is the expansion of people-smuggling networks, which are often linked to other forms of smuggling and organized crime. Smuggling routes are also highly dangerous: it is estimated that 2,000 people have died over the past decade trying to enter western Europe illegally.[31] Another aspect of the problem is the exploitation of migrants by traffickers: many trafficked migrants are forced to work in appalling conditions on farms or in sweatshops, catering or prostitution, often to pay back trafficking debts. Given the considerable risks and problems of illegal movement, it is not surprising that governments are keen to find ways to reduce the use of people-smuggling and -trafficking networks. And given the continued demand for low-skilled labour in sectors such as agriculture, catering and textiles, it seems wise to try to meet this demand through legal rather than illegal routes. Many European countries have therefore characterized new opportunities for economic migration as a means of cracking down on illegal migration and trafficking networks.

The link between the two is, however, open to challenge. The notion that expanded legal migration routes will lead to a reduction in the supply of illegal migrants assumes that there is a finite supply of illegal migrants, of which a proportion will be absorbed legally by new migration programmes, leaving a smaller number of irregular migrants. But it is also possible that expanding legal migration schemes could lead to an increase in the supply of potential migrants. According to some commentators, liberalizing rules on labour migration could raise expectations about the general availability of jobs, including irregular labour. An increase in legal migration could also consolidate existing networks, or create new ones, between resident migrants and their communities at home, generating chain migration. Thus although expanded possibilities for regular labour migration may encourage many potential illegal migrants to switch to legal routes, they are unlikely to be able to absorb all would-be migrants. The expansion of legal migration could create a 'pull' factor for increased numbers of illegal migrants. A second reason to question whether expanded legal immigration programmes will reduce illegal flows relates to the sources of demand for irregular labour. For some sectors, such as catering, textiles or small-scale agriculture, foreign labour may be affordable only if people are willing to accept below-minimum salaries without social payments. The use of irregular employees may reflect not simply a shortage of supply of legal employees, but a preference for employing illegal migrants.

Given these uncertainties about the impact of liberalization on irregular migration and employment, arguments based on this claimed linkage may be largely symbolic, or at the very least not sufficiently thought through. Defining an expansion of migration routes as a means of combating illegal migration may lend such policies more popular appeal, but it is less clear that they will be effective in reducing illegal immigration.

We have examined some of the main arguments supporting the liberalization of labour migration policy. How have these arguments and interests influenced policies in the UK, Germany and Italy?

### The UK: subtle but decisive change of course

The Labour government of Tony Blair has been particularly receptive to economic arguments for migration. This is in some ways paradoxical. As noted in Chapter 1, British administrations after the Second World War by and large failed to base migration policies on any serious analysis of economic or demographic needs. This was in contrast to most continental European countries, which were far more active in planning migration to meet labour demand. Nonetheless, the UK already had a number of provisions in place for meeting specific types of labour demand, before the reforms of the late 1990s. One of these was a scheme for seasonal agricultural labour dating back to the 1940s. In 2002, the scheme allowed up to 15,200 non-EEA students to work on farms for up to three months. Meanwhile a 'working holidaymakers scheme' permitted Commonwealth nationals to work in the UK for up to 18 months. In addition, the 1971 Immigration Act, while generally restricting migration, nonetheless allowed for the recruitment of a limited number of skilled employees from outside the EC. This was under the condition that the potential employer could demonstrate that the post could not be filled by an EC (subsequently EEA) national. The number of work permits issued remained fairly low until the mid- to late 1980s, with numbers peaking at 30,000 in 1990 and then falling back before rising again after 1994.[32] Most workers granted long-term permits were professional and managerial workers, mainly from other highly industrialized countries.[33]

In 1991, the work permit system was modified so as to exempt a number of selected categories from the labour market needs test. Workers linked to foreign investment projects, those on senior-level intra-company transfers and those filling posts at board level or equivalent were excluded from this requirement, as were workers in highly skilled occupations which were acknowledged to have an acute shortage of supply.[34] These changes were clearly linked to the sorts of pressures described earlier in the chapter: the importance of attracting MNCs and foreign investment, and gaps in the labour supply (although, interestingly, the definition of sectors with an acute supply shortfall was limited to the health sector, and did not include ICT until March 2000).[35] The procedure for all other categories remained cumbersome; firms were obliged to go through a lengthy procedure in order to justify recruitment of a non-EEA national. Moreover, the system was perceived as discouraging foreign investment, thereby undermining the UK's international competitiveness.

A number of pressures prompted the government to expand these provisions from 2000 onwards. Of crucial importance in determining these changes was the influence of business, especially the ICT sector, as well as pressure from the public sector (health services and education). The Labour government also appears to have undergone a fundamental shift in its thinking on migration issues. One consideration underlying this shift was the government's emphasis on the knowledge-based economy and the critical role of human capital in generating economic growth. The Labour government has consistently emphasized how essential education and skills are to economic success and, correspondingly, how skills gaps can hamper growth. As the February 2002 White Paper on 'Secure Borders, Safe Haven: Integration with Diversity in Modern Britain' acknowledged, 'developed economies are becoming more knowledge-based and more dependent on people with skills and ideas. Migrants bring new experiences and talents that can widen and enrich the knowledge base of the economy.'[36] Already in 1998, the government had established a National Skills Task Force (NSTF), chaired by the head of the British Chamber of Commerce, to advise it on labour market gaps. The NSTF stressed the need for additional ICT workers, a concern subsequently reflected in the Department for Trade and Industry's White Paper on 'Our Competitive Future: Building the Knowledge Economy'.[37]

Drawing on these ideas, the government made a number of proposals in 1999 for pilot projects designed to make immigration processes more business-friendly and to facilitate access for foreign entrepreneurs. In 2000 the work permit scheme was revised considerably, with reduced skills criteria for prospective employees and the inclusion of ICT in the acute shortage list. Overseas students who studied in the UK were also allowed to apply for work permits. Pilot schemes were introduced to facilitate intra-company transfers and to attract foreign entrepreneurs whose business plan would lead to 'exceptional economic benefit' to the UK.[38]

Of more symbolic significance, the government established a special programme, outside the existing work permit system, for attracting high-skilled workers. The Highly Skilled Migrant Programme, which started in January 2002, was designed to attract scientists, doctors, business and finance professionals to the UK. Applicants under the programme do not need to hold a post already in order to qualify for a permit but are instead assessed on a points system based on qualifications and experience. They may initially stay for a period of one year, extendable to three years, and then have the possibility of permanent residence. The February 2002 government White Paper on immigration advocated further changes, including expanded access to the labour market for postgraduate students.[39] The White Paper also made the case for loosening the rules on the migration of low-skilled people. It argued that there was 'a clear need for short-term casual labour' and suggested extending the seasonal agricultural workers' scheme to other sectors, and expanding the 'working holidaymakers' scheme to non-Commonwealth countries.[40]

Reaction in the UK to the new measures was surprisingly restrained. They received minimal press coverage and were embraced by the two main opposition parties. Given the highly politicized treatment of migration issues, how can we explain this moderate, non-partisan reaction? One reason was undoubtedly the general economic context: by 2000 the Labour government could boast the lowest level of unemployment since the pre-recession 1970s, with the unemployment rate down to around five per cent. Under these conditions, it was relatively uncontroversial to make the case for immigrants filling gaps in the labour market. Even the right-wing *Daily Telegraph* acknowledged that low-skilled migrants are 'useful, often doing the jobs that indigenous people don't want, particularly at a time of full employment'.[41]

Secondly, the measures were, in any case, targeted primarily at skilled workers. The case for recruiting highly qualified ICT staff, engineers or medical staff may well be easier to justify to the public. They fill urgent gaps in public services or stimulate the new economy. As the Confederation of British Industry estimated at the time, immigrants brought roughly £2.5 billion to the UK economy, especially those with high skills, and those who were complementary to native workers. This understanding of the benefits of skilled immigration was certainly a far cry from media images of 'bogus' asylum-seekers and illegal migrants.

The government also began to introduce a number of changes to provisions on low-skilled labour migrants in late 2002. In October 2002 it introduced a quota-based scheme to allow hotels and restaurants and food manufacturers to employ temporary migrant workers in areas where there were recruitment problems.[42] The following month it announced the expansion of the seasonal agricultural workers scheme, increasing the quota of non-EEA workers and loosening the criteria for their participation in the scheme.[43] Possible changes to the 'working holidaymakers' scheme were still under review in early 2003. At the same time, the Home Office has become more forthright in making a general case for both low- and high-skilled labour migration. In December 2002 it drew on commissioned research to argue that 'migrants bring a diversity of skills to the UK labour market, providing skills and expertise which complement the existing workforce. They do not increase unemployment among the domestic population, and may even increase wage levels.'[44]

However, the government has tended to be relatively more circumspect about liberalizing provisions on low-skilled labour than on those covering high-skilled labour. Schemes for low-skilled labour continue to be temporary, contract-based systems, which – unlike those for the highly skilled – do not offer possibilities for long-term settlement in the UK. Moreover, when expansion of unskilled labour migration is mentioned, it is usually depicted – perhaps somewhat disingenuously – as part of a solution to the problem of illegal migration. Thus the Home Secretary David Blunkett has characterized possible measures to expand low-skilled immigration as dealing 'a body blow to the gangmasters and people traffickers who bring people to this country illegally';[45] and the Home Office minister Beverly Hughes has argued that 'properly managed migration helps tackle illegal working and abuse of the asylum system'.[46] We have seen earlier why this claim is open to serious doubt. Yet this type of 'packaging' of labour migration policies, together with tough rhetoric on illegal immigrants and asylum-seekers, appear to have become features of the government's strategy for winning support for the liberalized provisions. Statements and proposals on expanding labour migration have been consistently presented alongside announcements about new measures to crack down on asylum-seekers, migrant-trafficking and illegal immigrants (see Chapter 3 for a more detailed discussion of this question).

Another factor favouring this more pro-immigrant agenda is an unusual degree of cross-party consensus on the need for (at least skilled) labour migration. Unlike its continental counterparts, the Conservative Party embraces an essentially neo-liberal, anti-protectionist ideology and has a natural affinity with this business-friendly agenda. Anti-immigrant mobilization has tended to be targeted at those migrants who are seen as an economic burden – asylum-seekers and illegal immigrants – rather than at productive, highly skilled migrants. The Liberal Democrats have meanwhile tended to be more supportive of liberal policies on both immigration and asylum than the Labour government.

The openness to economically productive migrants versus 'burdensome' ones also has much to do with patterns of UK discourse on what are considered to be legitimate and illegitimate criteria for including certain categories of migrants. Mainstream political parties are, by and large, keen to avoid anti-migration arguments explicitly based on ethnocentric grounds. Thus arguments linked to problems of cultural difference are widely stigmatized as racist, and mainstream parties are careful to couch objections to immigration in more utilitarian terms. In this context, attempts to make the case for economically beneficial labour migration to the UK have not (at least to date) run up against the kinds of cultural arguments seen in Germany that are based on concerns about integration or social cohesion.

The government has therefore benefited from a number of favourable conditions: low unemployment, no significant party political opposition and a generally supportive public discourse which is relatively receptive to the case for economically productive immigration. Under these circumstances, decisions on recruiting economically beneficial labour migrants may well continue to generate elite consensus and, as such, be largely kept off the political agenda. In this sense, we may be seeing a partial shift to a postwar continental model of labour migration policy. As Chapter 3 shows, this could occur at the expense of other categories of migrants. Arguably, provisions to liberalize skilled or non-skilled labour migration may be acceptable only as part of a more restrictive package designed to protect nationals from other types of migration 'threats'.

### Germany: explicit reassessment

The debate on immigration policy reform in Germany has been far more prominent and contentious. As in the UK, it was a centre-left government, Chancellor Gerhard Schröder's SPD–Green coalition, that introduced more flexible rules on migration. Schröder launched a so-called 'Green Card' scheme in 2000 designed to attract additional ICT workers, largely in response to pressure from business. This scheme and the subsequent *Zuwanderungs-gesetz* (Migration Law) were widely seen as representing a significant break with Germany's hitherto restrictive migration policy.

However, as in the UK case, it is not entirely correct to characterize this as a volte-face. In the early 1990s Germany had begun to recruit seasonal and contract labour through bilateral schemes with central and east European countries. In 1999 the seasonal labour scheme admitted around 223,400 workers, mostly Polish nationals, for maximum periods of three months.[47] Legislation also permitted the recruitment of contract workers, whose numbers stood at around 30–40,000 per year in the late 1990s.[48] The Foreigners Law of 1990, meanwhile, allowed for exceptions to the general ban on immigration, which were subsequently applied to two categories of workers – senior staff of MNCs and other highly skilled workers – on the condition that their recruitment was in the 'public interest'. But the conditions and procedures for recruiting this second category were cumbersome and restrictive, involving a case-by-case assessment based on labour needs as well as on more general economic, social and political interests.[49] This was perceived to penalize smaller firms, which were unable to benefit from the more streamlined procedure for MNC personnel, and thus to impede the expansion of the ICT sector as a whole.[50] This contributed in turn to concerns that Germany was lagging behind other states in the development of ICT and was failing to attract workers from the limited international pool of ICT specialists.

The 2000 scheme was designed to redress this imbalance, providing a more flexible route for recruiting ICT specialists. The establishment of the 'Green Card' scheme was announced in February 2000 at an ICT trade fair organized by the Confederation for Information Technology, Telecommunications and New Media (Bitkom) following claims by Bitkom that the ICT sector faced a shortage of 75,000 workers. Athough the Federal Labour Office questioned this estimate, it shared the general concern about the insufficient development of ICT and consulted employers in the preparation of provisions under the new initiative. The 'Green Card' scheme aimed to attract up to 20,000 specialists to stay for a period of up to five years. It was envisaged that most would be drawn from central and eastern Europe, reflecting a general preference for European migrants, although in subsequent debates specialists from India were also referred to as potential candidates. The government was, however, keen to emphasize its continued concern about domestic unemployment: employers would need to demonstrate that they could not find an EEA expert for the job. At the same time the government announced the expansion of its placement scheme for German ICT trainees.[51]

The government also introduced changes to provisions on unskilled labour, although these have been less prominent in the media. A decree of December 2000 allowed asylum-seekers to enter the labour market after one year, and the government announced plans to extend seasonal and temporary labour schemes to the nationals of central and east European countries. Interestingly, however, the German government also backed the introduction of a seven-year moratorium on the right to free movement of nationals of central and east European countries once they had acceded to the European Union. It therefore stopped short of a more expansive liberalization of labour flows as accepted by some other EU states; the emphasis remained on the management of migration flows according to predefined labour needs.

The German government has had a far harder time selling these changes than its British counterpart. It has come under fire from a number of directions. Business, migrant groups, trade unions and left-wing parties have claimed that the changes do not go far enough, and have been especially critical of the five-year limit on work permits. Meanwhile, although the CDU and the CSU were initially fairly supportive of the 'Green Card' initiative, the issue of whether Germany should liberalize restrictions on migration has become a major area of division between government and opposition. The Christian Democratic parties' joint candidate for chancellor for the 2002 elections, the CSU's Edmund Stoiber, criticized the moves as giving priority to provisions encouraging the immigration of foreign workers over measures to expand training opportunities for German nationals.[52] He and other party members also linked the debate on increasing labour migration to the question of integration and cultural identity, which had become a major subject of party political debate in Germany since the late 1990s (see Chapter 4). The CDU and CSU parties argued that questions of integration should be clarified before Germany let in large numbers of additional immigrants.

Partly to respond to the wider issues raised by the labour migration debate, in 2001 the government established the independent *Zuwanderungskommission* (Migration Commission), headed by the moderate CDU parliamentarian Rita Süssmuth and composed of a range of specialists, politicians, employers, unions, NGOs and religious and migrant groups. The Commission's influential final report, *Zuwanderung gestalten, Integration fördern* ('Structuring Migration, Fostering Integration'), was published in July 2001. It argued for the need to expand labour migration, on three main grounds: the growing importance of qualifications and knowledge for competitiveness in the global economy; the problem of Germany's ageing population; and existing gaps in the labour supply.[53] Significantly, it stressed the need to recognize that Germany was an immigration country, reversing a long-standing self-depiction of it as *kein Einwanderungsland* ('not a country of immigration').

The Süssmuth Commission recommended four main channels for meeting the demand for foreign labour. The first was a points system based on qualifications, skills and other criteria (similar to Canadian and UK schemes) which would grant permanent residence to successful applicants. The second was shorter-term permits of up to five years for sectors such as ICT where there was a labour shortage, but with a subsequent possibility for migrants to be granted permanent residence through the proposed points system. Thirdly, it suggested expanding the opportunities for foreign students to come to study or train in Germany, allowing them the possibility to receive a residence permit after they had completed their course. Finally, the Commission's report proposed a new category, for top staff and specialists with high salaries in industry and science; they could also enter on one- to five-year permits, potentially extendable through the points system.

The government incorporated many of these recommendations into its new draft law. For the first time the legislation covered matters of residence, employment and integration of foreigners in one integrated law. The proposed law significantly simplified the system of permits, reducing it to the two statuses of permanent and temporary residence, and streamlined applications into a single procedure for granting residence and work permits. Following the general direction of the Süssmuth Commission's recommendations, high-skilled workers such as those in ICT, engineers, scientists

43

and researchers would have the possibility of applying for permanent residence from the outset. In addition, graduates of German universities were entitled to a residence permit for one year, during which time they could seek employment.

The bill was rather more cautious in embracing the idea of a points system. It established the possibility of a quota for skilled migrants based on pre-set criteria, but stressed that this would be restricted to very limited numbers, if used at all. The bill also established a Federal Office for Migration and Refugees, whose tasks were to include coordinating information on labour migrants and administering the points system and integration.

The SPD Interior Minister, Otto Schily, worked hard to secure support for the bill. He had to make concessions both to the SPD's more progressive coalition partner, the Green Party, and to the more conservative CDU–CSU opposition. Part of his strategy was to generate broad social consensus for the proposals, especially by enlisting the support of the social partners (trade unions and employers).[54] But the CDU–CSU remained critical of the bill, cautioning against liberalizing migration without effectively addressing problems of integration, asylum 'abuse' and family reunion. In the course of compromise negotiations with the Christian Democratic parties, the government changed a number of aspects of the bill, introducing more restrictive provisions on family reunion, asylum and integration. Attempts to amend the bill failed to satisfy the opposition, raising government fears that it would become a central campaigning issue in the September 2002 elections. Lack of opposition support also meant that the bill was blocked in March 2002 by the upper chamber, the Bundesrat, where the government coalition parties had a majority of just one.[55]

Despite the heated debate over the passing of the new law, immigration did not play a major role in the national elections in September 2002. In fact, political commentators were surprised at the low level of support for far-right anti-immigrant parties and the apparent lack of public interest in immigration questions.

The future of German migration policy therefore remains very much in the balance. A number of factors have made the introduction of more liberal labour migration policies far more contested than in the British case. One factor is the problem of higher unemployment in Germany and the centre-right opposition's readiness to pursue a stance that is more protectionist of the labour market. The CDU and the CSU have been more willing and able to marshal arguments about labour migration posing a threat to native workers than has their British Conservative Party counterpart. A second factor is that German voters may well be more cautious about the notion of using labour migration as a tool of economic policy, in view of the lessons learned from the guest-worker era. Moreover, Germany has been less ready than the UK to embrace a self-image as a multicultural society. Thus despite the strong economic case for high-skilled immigration, there are continued concerns about the impact of additional immigration on German identity. Such concerns have been more openly expressed than in the UK, where public debate on questions about cultural diversity is more constrained by fears about the impact of an exclusionist discourse on race relations and by political parties' interest in wooing ethnic minority voters.

In short, the Christian Democratic opposition has attempted to mobilize public concerns about employment and collective identity to oppose labour migration, despite the evident economic benefits of such an approach. It remains questionable, though, whether the essentially business-friendly Christian Democratic parties will retain this position if they gain power in the next national elections.

## Italy: between labour demand and security concerns

Since it first introduced legislation to control migration in the 1980s, Italy has kept open a number of channels for regular labour migration. As indicated in Chapter 1, Italy began to receive significant levels of immigration only in the 1970s, but between the mid-1980s and 2000 its foreign population increased from around 300,000 to 1.46 million.[56] This figure excludes irregular migrants, whose number is estimated to have grown from around 272,000 in 1980 to 1.25 million in 1998.[57] A series of laws in the 1980s and 1990s sought to manage flows, and especially to crack down on the number of illegal immigrants, through tougher measures on entry and stay. But from the outset Italian policy has been somewhat ambivalent in its quest for restriction. Not only has it kept open a quota for legal migrants but it has also – more paradoxically from the point of view of deterring illegal immigrants – offered regular amnesties for illegal immigrants already in Italy.

Unlike in the UK and Germany, then, there has been no discernible shift in Italian policy from one aiming at 'zero immigration' to an explicit acknowledgment of the need for migrant labour. Rather, since the 1980s Italy has been trying to juggle substantial demand for low-skilled immigrant labour with pressures for restriction. These pressures emanate both from sections of domestic public opinion and from other EU and Schengen countries, which are concerned that Italy is a 'soft touch' for illegal migrants entering the EU. This tension between economic demand for labour and political pressure for restriction has often produced inconsistent and incoherent policy outcomes.

The demand for immigrant labour is strongest in the industrial north of the country, where many small and medium-sized enterprises are dependent on immigrants. In 1999–2000 the recruitment of non-EEA immigrant workers accounted for 34.8 per cent of the total legal recruitment in the northeast of the country and for 51.2 per cent of the recruitment of unskilled personnel.[58] This implies a massive dependence on foreign labour, especially in the sectors of manual trades, tourism, agriculture, construction, domestic services and home care. Although unemployment levels remain at 21 per cent in the south (compared to 5.7 per cent in the centre and north of the country), there is limited internal labour mobility. Employers have therefore put pressure on successive governments to expand opportunities for legal immigration, pushing for larger annual quotas as well as for schemes to facilitate the integration of migrants into the labour market.[59]

The case for labour migration has also been influenced by fears about ageing populations. Demographic projections show that Italy will be especially badly hit by this problem in coming decades. The Italian birth rate is one of the lowest in Europe, at 1.2 per female. Many pensioners are already dependent on immigrants for health care and domestic help, and are likely to resist any moves to limit this supply.[60] Even though many commentators have argued that immigration cannot be a tool for addressing the problem of rising dependency rates, immediate shortages in sectors such as domestic and health care work are likely to exert considerable pressure on Italian governments of any political hue to loosen migration provisions.

Since the 1980s, Italy has responded to the demand for foreign labour by introducing various laws and decrees in order to ensure a supply of legal migrant labour. The main instrument for recruiting this labour has been a series of amnesties or regularizations of irregular migrants already in Italy; programmes were introduced in 1982, 1986, 1990, 1997, 1998 and 2000. The programmes in the 1990s each regularized around 230,000–250,000 migrants.[61] They were criticized by the right-wing Polo delle Libertà parties (subsequently Casa delle Libertà), which include the anti-immigration parties Forza Italia, Alleanza Nazionale and the Lega Nord. Nonetheless, consecutive centre-left governments in the 1990s continued to pursue a relatively flexible policy vis-à-vis labour migrants. Legislation in 1986 had already allowed for the recruitment of foreign workers if no Italian workers were available to fill jobs. Subsequent legislation in July 1998 under the centre-left Ulivo coalition – the so-called 'Single Act' – introduced a quota system for immigration, which was to be set annually on the basis of labour market needs. The quota for 1999 was 53,000, rising to 63,000 in 2000 and 83,000 in 2001. In addition, there were quotas for seasonal workers, of whom there were around 20,000 in 2000. These quotas have been filled by a combination of regularizations of those already present in Italy and new arrivals, including those entering each year under bilateral schemes with

Albania (6,000 migrants), Tunisia (3,000) and Morocco (3,000). The Single Act also established the category of *lavoro autonomo*, a work permit for subcontracted and cooperative labour, and a new job-seeker's visa, which provided work permits for job-seekers who were sponsored by private individuals, firms or municipalities. The legislation included the possibility of permanent residence for documented migrants after five years' legal residence.

Unlike in many other west European countries, the Italian public appears to have been relatively unperturbed about possible negative repercussions of labour migration on welfare, unemployment or wages. Polls show that most people do not see immigrants as being in competition with locals for jobs; there is a widespread recognition that foreigners are mainly doing jobs that Italians do not want.[62] Instead, anti-immigration rhetoric is sharply focused on questions of criminality and security. The persistent problem of illegal entry into Italy since the early 1990s has seriously undermined public confidence in the state's capacity to manage its borders.[63]

Successive governments have attempted to combat this problem through stepping up border patrols and introducing stricter measures on detention and deportation. However, there has been widespread dissatisfaction with the apparent inability of centre-left governments to tackle the problem effectively. The popular media and right-wing parties were highly critical of the record of centre-left governments in the 1990s, especially their failure to implement more deportations or to intercept and better control illegal arrivals. Public acceptance of the traditional mainstream parties' more moderate stance on immigration was certainly not aided by the corruption scandals which exploded onto the political scene in 1992–3. The scandals discredited both of the main postwar centrist political parties – the Democrazia Cristiana (Christian Democrats) and the Partito Socialista Italiano (or Italian Socialist Party) – along with many of the more moderate policies they had espoused (see Chapter 4).

Fears about immigration and security have been linked not only to illegal entry but also, increasingly, to perceptions about criminality among the immigrant population. Since the early 1990s there have been widespread concerns, articulated by a predominantly anti-immigrant populist media, that immigrants are responsible for rising crime in the northern regions.[64] Immigrants from the Balkans, and particularly Albania, are widely believed to be involved in organized crime, with links with Italy's own mafia.[65] Surveys have suggested that 75 per cent of Italians believe that immigration and crime are directly linked.[66] It is these perceived linkages between immigration, crime and security that appear to be the main obstacle to expanding or even sustaining existing provisions on the recruitment of labour migrants. Since the early 1990s, right-wing parties have mobilized support by linking rising crime rates in northern Italy to an increase in immigration and promising to introduce tougher measures to address the problem. This resolve to tackle illegal immigration has impacted on policies on legal labour migration, as will be discussed below.

This might seem surprising, given the strongly neo-conservative, pro-business orientation suggested by much of Berlusconi's rhetoric. One might have expected a combination of tough rhetoric on illegal migrants, combined with a business-friendly policy towards regular labour migrants. Such a distinction has at times been embraced even by the far-right Lega Nord – in the words of one of its deputies, Italy should 'let in only those who come to work, not those who come to commit crime'.[67] It is also apparent in the Labour and Social Policy Ministry's thinking under the Berlusconi administration. A White Paper on 'The Labour Market in Italy' of October 2001, for example, emphasizes the benefits of immigrant labour, which, it argues, is complementary to the skills and preferences of indigenous workers. At the same time it stresses the need for tighter control over illegal flows.[68]

However, it appears that the electoral dividends of sending out a clear, unnuanced anti-immigration message were too tempting for the right-wing coalition government. Once in power, the new Casa delle Libertà coalition introduced the Bossi-Fini Law, which included measures to restrict both illegal and legal labour migration. The legislation, which came into force in July 2002, predictably tightened provisions on deportation, increased the penalties for illegal migration and restricted access to asylum. It also considerably tightened provisions on legal labour migration. The new law abolished the possibility for immigrants to enter legally to seek work and removed the sponsorship system established under the 1998 law. Employers recruiting workers from abroad were given responsibility for arranging their accommodation and also for covering the costs of their deportation, if necessary. The residence status of migrant workers was made conditional on their employment status, implying that any labour migrant who lost his or her job would automatically become illegal, with a toleration period of six months prior to expulsion. Meanwhile, the average length for residence permits was reduced, so that renewals of permits would be granted for two instead of four years. The renewal must be requested 90 days in advance (rather than 30, as under the previous legislation). Other more restrictive provisions included extension of the minimum period of residence before non-EU citizens could apply for permanent residence status (*carta di soggiorno*) from five to six years, as well as stricter rules on family reunion.

In a small gesture to business requirements, the entry quota system remained in place, although it was set at 59,000 for 2002, in contrast to 83,000 for the previous year. Moreover, despite the governing coalition parties' strident critique of regularization programmes in the 1990s, the government has continued to offer amnesties. A September 2002 amnesty regularized the status of domestic workers and certain other categories of employees. The introduction of the programme was largely a response to pressure from business and employers' associations, which were keen to ensure a source of immigrant labour.

The maintenance of the regularization system is paradoxical given the government's apparently tough stance on illegal immigration and its professed goal of limiting labour migration. It implies a highly ambivalent approach to migration policy: on the one hand, an explicitly restrictive approach through legislative provisions; on the other, measures which allow thousands of illegal entrants to stay, almost certainly creating a 'pull' factor for future illegal migrants.[69] Thus whereas the UK and Germany have been keen to keep flows of illegal and legal migrants separate, being anxious to avoid drawing on illegal immigrants as a source of legal labour migration, Italy appears to be doing precisely the opposite.

The Bossi-Fini law met considerable resistance from business and employers' associations. The head of Italy's main employers' federation, Confindustria, complained that 'Italian industry can't survive without the help of immigrant workers', while the president of the parliamentary industrial committee argued that the new law would be a disaster for the economy, leading to a 'haemorrhage' of the workforce required for economic growth.[70] Of particular concern for business was the law's linkage of residence permits to work permits, which was seen as impeding flexibility and labour mobility, particularly in seasonal jobs such as agriculture. Business and employers' groups have also criticized the 2002 regularization programme for not going far enough. Especially vocal were employers in the Veneto region, who complained that the scheme did not allow for the regularization of employees who had already received a deportation order.

Berlusconi and his government appear to have been sensitive to these criticisms from business. Indeed, objections to the regularization programme prompted Berlusconi to promise to revise the clause excluding migrants with deportation orders. As we saw, these criticisms also pressured the government into retaining an annual quota for labour migration, albeit one that was considerably smaller than the quota for 2002. However, Forza Italia remains under considerable pressure from the even more pro-restriction and populist Lega Nord. Umberto Bossi and his party have been arguing that the Bossi-Fini law does not go far enough in restricting migration, and the party has dismissed business concerns about labour supply, declaring that the government 'made a pact with the voters, not with industry'.[71] While the Lega Nord's inclusion in the coalition is not essential to the government's survival,

Berlusconi appears to be keen to keep it on board, probably to limit its scope for populist mobilization against government policies.

Strong opposition has also come from centre and left parties, trade unions and the Catholic Church. Much of their critique has focused on the humanitarian implications of the law and its impact on public attitudes towards immigration. The law's provisions on the fingerprinting of all non-EU entrants was particularly controversial and was criticized as being highly discriminatory. Left-wing parties have accused the law of pandering to racist views, while unions have argued that it places labour migrants in a highly vulnerable position.[72]

In sum, Italian policy debate in the 1980s and 1990s continued to recognize the economic benefits of immigration. But the phenomenon of irregular migration has come to be seen as a major threat to security and has been used as a central issue in campaigns by the far right, especially in the north of Italy. The appeal of this type of anti-immigrant rhetoric was clearly boosted by the collapse of the mainstream parties in 1992 and by the failure of centre-left coalitions to be seen to tackle the problem effectively. But the tough stance on immigration has also filtered through to policies on labour migration, to the consternation of business and employers' groups and trade unions. It appears that the new restrictions may be partly offset by continued regularization programmes. Ironically, this will almost certainly make Italy more attractive as a destination for illegal migrants, keeping alive the sense of crisis and lack of control that has fed resistance to expanding legal migration to Italy.

### CONCLUSION: THE SUSTAINABILITY OF NEW LABOUR MIGRATION POLICIES

Predictably enough, the main impetus for more liberal labour migration policies has come from business groups and liberal, pro-business political parties in all three countries under analysis. Centre-left governments in both the UK and Germany have advanced an economic case for migration based on the need to fill specific gaps in the labour market. The UK has been especially keen to stress the need to compete for highly qualified personnel in the new knowledge-based economy, while Germany has thus far focused on specific gaps in the ICT sector. In Italy, by contrast, neither previous centre-left governments nor the current right-wing coalition have taken a strong position in defence of labour migration, although both have tolerated it in practice through quotas, regularizations and a failure to crack down more effectively on illegal immigrants. The most vocal supporters of labour migration have been the social partners.

Demographic arguments have not been prominent in the reasoning of any of the three governments – probably because politicians are cautious about appearing to embrace a policy of replacement migration rather than considering alternative options such as expanding training programmes, or reforms to retirement practices and pension systems. However, one can expect the demographic case to be made more forcefully by business and centre-left parties as labour shortages become more acute in the coming years and decades.

The pressures constraining this economically driven agenda vary quite substantially between countries. Party politics play a very important role here. The British government has been in the favourable position of facing no significant resistance to its labour migration reforms, at least to date. This may change as demographic pressures force the government to consider a more radical expansion of channels for legal migration by low-skilled workers. Moreover, until now the government has been clever in packaging these reforms with more high-profile restrictive measures for asylum-seekers and illegal migrants. However, it is not clear whether this tactic will remain open to them for future labour migration reforms: there are limits to the palette of restrictionist measures available in liberal democratic states.

The German government has faced relatively greater problems with the CDU–CSU opposition, which combines a generally pro-business stance with a protectionist approach to welfare, employment and, not least, cultural identity. Much of the CDU–CSU's critique of the Migration Law may be interpreted as populistic posturing, which would almost certainly be toned down should these parties find themselves in office. Resistance to labour migration also reflects the relatively recent realization in Germany that it is a mistake to view immigration simply as an instrument of economic policy: it has far wider socio-economic and cultural repercussions.

Italy's greatest obstacle to a more open labour migration policy has derived from the strong public preoccupation with illegal migration. This has encouraged right-wing political parties to compete for electoral support by promising more effective migration control and restriction. This agenda has filtered into policy on legal labour migration. Meanwhile, the centre-left has failed to make a convincing distinction between the need to tackle illegal migration and the economic case for managed labour migration. Its focus on humanitarian arguments, important as these may be, has contributed to a polarization of the debate into one between well-meaning ethical liberals and Catholic groups, and more pragmatic restrictionists. The main lobby for labour migration has come from the social partners, who have had some influence in revising or moderating government measures. The critical issue for the future of labour migration policy appears to be whether these humanitarian and business arguments can prevail over populist anti-immigration opinion.

# 3

# Asylum-seekers and illegal immigrants

The emerging labour migration agenda raises a number of questions about the impact of new migration policies on other categories of migrants. Some commentators have argued that the increasing demand for labour migrants will have a generally liberalizing effect on migration and asylum policies as a whole.[1] Others have suggested that it might usher in a new era of clientelist migration policy-making, with political consensus effectively taking migration off the party political agenda.[2] In both cases, the assumption is that the rising demand for labour migration could imply a return to a pre-1970s model in which most would-be immigrants or refugees would be absorbed through legal migration schemes without significant public debate or resistance.

But there are grounds for questioning whether this will really be the case. One reason to be sceptical is purely practical: asylum-seekers and illegal immigrants will not necessarily have the skills corresponding to current or future labour market gaps. Even if they do, governments are likely to be cautious about drawing on them as a source of labour. Asylum is an expensive route for labour recruitment and is difficult to control. Moreover, recruiting labour through the asylum system or from already resident illegal immigrants would probably create incentives for potential economic migrants to enter west European countries illegally or through the asylum route. By and large, governments may be keen to avoid encouraging the idea that an asylum application is an easy route to legal employment.[3]

Related to this is a more political reason why liberal migration policies – where they emerge at all – are unlikely to have a positive knock-on effect for asylum-seekers or illegal migrants.[4] Since the 1980s both groups have been systematically stigmatized by sections of the popular media and more populist political parties. Asylum-seekers and irregular migrants have been linked to problems of unemployment, overstretched welfare systems, rising criminality and internal insecurity. This has often, though not exclusively, been in supposed contrast to tax-paying legal immigrants or ethnic minorities. This pattern of exclusion of asylum-seekers and illegal migrants does not appear to be disappearing with the emergence of new, pro-labour migration policies. On the contrary, there are indications that more liberal labour migration policies are being packaged with guarantees of stricter measures to clamp down on asylum-seekers and illegal migrants.

This chapter will look at the relationship between new migration policies and the treatment of asylum-seekers and illegal immigrants. The first two sections will examine how and why the current treatment of these two groups emerged, tracing the growth of anti-asylum and anti-illegal immigrant sentiment in west European states. The third section will consider how this pattern of exclusion is influencing the debate on the new migration policies discussed in Chapter 2. One can trace different patterns of debate in the three countries under analysis. In the cases of Germany and the UK, rather than implying generally more liberal treatment of all categories of immigrants, the new policies are for the most part kept separate from continued restrictive policies on asylum-seekers and illegal immigrants. Indeed, new migration policies have partly been justified by promises to strengthen controls on asylum-seekers and illegal immigrants, especially in the UK. Italy is a somewhat divergent case: the failure to draw a sharp distinction between questions of regular labour migration and problems of illegal migration control has led to a more confused debate in which responses to the two phenomena have become conflated.

### THE ASYLUM 'CRISIS'

The asylum issue began to emerge as a major problem in western Europe from the mid-1970s onwards. As shown in Chapter 1, before that decade the practice of granting asylum had been underpinned by a combination of Cold War ideological motives and humanitarian commitment, in a context of economic growth and small numbers of mainly European refugees. This had created elite consensus in most societies regarding the need for relatively generous asylum provisions. But from the 1970s onwards these conditions began to change.

First, this period saw a significant rise in the number of people seeking asylum in Europe. One reason for the increase was a wave of 'new refugees' in Africa and Asia, fleeing civil conflict or repressive regimes. Cheaper travel possibilities and better information on travel routes and conditions in countries of destination also facilitated access to west European countries for nationals of many countries in Africa, Asia, the Middle East and South America. The new ethnic composition of asylum-seekers was unsettling for many receiving countries, especially at a time of sensitive public debate on the integration of economic migrants from previous decades. The predominance of refugees from Africa and Asia also confounded the accepted notion of refugees as dissidents from communism in east European countries. These asylum-seekers were no longer victims of communist repression but were what became dismissively referred to as 'economic migrants'.

(2) Secondly, increasingly negative reactions to asylum-seekers were influenced as much as anything by the growing perception of abuses of asylum systems. With the closure of legal routes for immigration in the 1970s, many would-be economic immigrants began to try to enter west European states through the asylum route. In many EC countries this entitled them to free accommodation, welfare benefits, access to social services, and a legal process for examining applications that could extend over years. Particular European countries began to obtain a reputation for offering good prospects for longer-term residence via the asylum route. Germany was one of the most popular, with its Basic Law granting multiple rights of appeal to asylum-seekers, implying that the process could last eight years or more. By this time, even if their applications were rejected, asylum-seekers would normally be allowed to stay on humanitarian grounds. The possibility that these provisions could be abused by non-genuine refugees led to fundamental doubts about the purpose and function of asylum systems, and appeared to undermine the humanitarian argument for granting asylum.

(3) Thirdly, the economic context was changing. Economic depression and rising unemployment were raising questions about the absorption capacity of receiving states. This made west European publics especially sensitive to the problem of the abuse of asylum systems. In this context, the media and some political parties began to challenge west European commitments to asylum-seekers. Accusations of asylum abuse or 'bogus' applications were more or less explicitly used in public debate, ostensibly legitimizing more restrictive measures.

## Germany: asylum 'crisis' and constitutional reform

These tendencies were particularly pronounced in the case of West Germany, which experienced a substantial rise in the numbers seeking asylum from the mid-1970s onwards – from just over 5,000 per year in the early 1970s to over 51,000 by 1978, with a peak of almost 108,000 in 1980. This rendered existing arrangements for the reception of asylum-seekers unworkable. Before 1974 all asylum-seekers had been accommodated in one centre in Bavaria, but from 1974 onwards the *Bundesländer* agreed to disperse asylum-seekers among them. One consequence was that the *Länder* now had to shoulder the costs of reception, welfare and social assistance. They therefore became increasingly vocal in calling for more restrictive measures to limit the numbers of asylum-seekers and the costs of supporting them. Meanwhile, the composition of asylum-seekers changed markedly, with an increasing proportion of applicants from non-communist countries. In the early 1970s the main countries of origin had been central and east European, especially Czechoslovakia, Hungary and Yugoslavia. By the second half of the 1970s the most significant countries of origin were Turkey, Pakistan, India, Lebanon, Ghana and Bangladesh.[5] When in 1980 the number of asylum applications rose above 100,000, over half were from Turkey, fuelling claims that the asylum system was being used as a route for economic migration.

The asylum question became a central topic of public debate in 1980, the principal question being that of how to prevent *Scheinasylanten* or 'bogus asylum-seekers' from abusing generous West German welfare and judicial provisions. At this stage, mainstream politicians were keen to stress that they were not opposed to granting protection and assistance to genuine asylum-seekers: they were simply against those entering for economic reasons. This distinction between so-called bona fide and 'non-genuine' applicants was to be a prominent feature of subsequent debates in West Germany and other European countries.

The government responded with measures to make entry more difficult and to discourage asylum abuse by lowering standards of social assistance for applicants. One initial measure restricted access to West German territory, with a new visa requirement imposed on Turkish nationals travelling to the country. Bonn also entered into negotiations with East Germany in order to prevent large numbers of asylum-seekers from entering via East Berlin. Legislation in 1982 modified reception conditions for asylum-seekers in West Germany, formalizing the existing system of dispersal between *Länder*, reducing social conditions for asylum-seekers, and banning their employment. Many of the provisions, such as the ban on work, collective accommodation and dispersal, appeared to be designed more to deter applicants than to reduce costs.[6] The law also streamlined the application procedure, reducing the possibilities for appealing against a negative decision and narrowing the definition of refugee.

The number of applicants declined over the next few years, only to rise again in the mid-1980s. From 1989 onwards, however, the problems of immigration and asylum began to take on dimensions that generated a sense of national crisis. After the removal of barriers to emigration in former communist states, large numbers of ethnic Germans from central and eastern Europe (*Aussiedler*), as well as many from East Germany (*Übersiedler*), settled in West Germany. Germany also received by far the largest number of refugees from the conflict in the former Yugoslavia. All in all, it absorbed around three million immigrants between 1989 and 1992, and this at a time of radical political and economic upheaval linked to reunification. Shifting ideological cleavages and notions of collective identity provided a context in which political groups were competing to mobilize support around new concepts of identity and membership.

At the same time, insecurity about socio-economic changes in the 'new' (former East German) *Länder* provided fertile ground for inciting hostility towards immigrants, and especially asylum-seekers. The unification treaty incorporated the new *Länder* into the asylum dispersal system, and the sudden arrival of asylum-seekers in areas without any experience of immigration, proved a target for outbreaks of violence. The two most dramatic incidents occurred in Hoyerswerda, Saxony in 1991 and in Rostock in 1992, when local residents attacked centres accommodating asylum-seekers.

The combination of increasing flows and growing xenophobia and racist violence led to the widespread perception that Germany was experiencing an asylum and immigration crisis. There was felt to be a need for robust measures in order to regain Germany's sovereignty in the area of migration and also to bring its provisions on asylum and immigration in line with those of other EU states.[7] Most of the resulting reforms focused on the asylum problem. First, and most significantly, came the repeal in 1993 of Germany's generous constitutional provisions on asylum. The famous December 1992 *Asylkompromiss* between the main political parties (excluding the Greens) established provisions for asylum-seekers who had travelled through 'safe' third countries to be returned to those countries. The Asylum Procedure Law of 1993 also introduced a special accelerated procedure for applicants from so-called safe countries of origin. This marked a significant shift, effectively breaking the taboo on revising Germany's postwar commitment to refugee protection. In the following years, Germany made use of this provision by signing a series of readmission agreements with neighbouring 'safe' countries that allowed it to return asylum-seekers who had travelled through their territory before illegally crossing into Germany. Legislation in 1997 and 1998 further limited assistance and rights for asylum-seekers.

The formula of restricting access to the asylum system, reducing social conditions for asylum-seekers and streamlining asylum procedures had two major, and for the most part unintended, consequences. First, it increased the social and economic marginalization of asylum-seekers. Most were accommodated in special reception centres or collective housing, with limited social benefits or assistance in kind and no entitlement to work. The concentration of large numbers of ethnic minority groups with limited resources and no employment increased their social exclusion and made them an easy target for resentment. Treatment of this group contrasted to the gradual incorporation of long-term residents and ethnic Germans. Secondly, as we shall see later in this chapter, the tightening of provisions first for labour migration and then for asylum systems foreclosed the possibilities for legal entry into Germany, almost certainly generating an increase in the number of those entering, staying and working in Germany on an illegal basis.

## The UK: storm in a teacup?

Although the UK did not experience anything like the rise in asylum applications seen in West Germany, the debate on immigration policy since the mid-1980s has focused almost exclusively on the asylum issue, intertwined with the problem of illegal entry. Until 1989 the level of asylum applications in the UK remained below 5,000 per year, less than one-tenth of the average number of applicants in West Germany over the same period. Nonetheless, concerns about asylum came to the fore in 1985, following a rise in the number of asylum-seekers from Sri Lanka: there were 1,893 applications, as compared to 548 the previous year. The Conservative government reacted with a series of measures to limit the possibilities for entering the UK. It imposed a visa requirement on Sri Lankan nationals in 1985, followed in 1986 by visa requirements for those travelling from India, Pakistan, Bangladesh, Nigeria and Ghana. In 1987 the government introduced the Immigration (Carrier's Liability) Act, which imposed penalties on airline and shipping companies carrying passengers without valid travel documents.

It is not easy to understand the level of furore over this relatively low number of asylum-seekers. As suggested in Chapter 1, the growing politicization of immigration since the 1970s can be understood in part in the context of more general popular anxieties about Britain's political and economic decline and the drastic economic restructuring and welfare state reforms of the 1980s. The Conservative government was successful in channelling some of these concerns into the problem of immigrants. And, as in the German case, when the number of asylum-seekers began to increase, it provided an obvious target for anti-immigrant sentiment.

The number of asylum applicants began to rise more substantially in the late 1980s, and in response the focus of British policy shifted to reform of the asylum procedure and reception conditions for asylum-seekers. The 1988 Immigration Act and the 1993 Asylum and Immigration Appeals Act aimed to streamline application procedures, allowing for an accelerated procedure for 'manifestly unfounded' asylum applications and removing the right to appeal in some cases. The legislation led to a sharp decline in the number of asylum-seekers granted refugee status or some other form of protection.

Prior to 1993 only around 16 per cent of all applicants were refused any sort of protection, but in 1994 the proportion of refusals rose to 75 per cent.[8] Nonetheless, the fall in the recognition rate had no discernible impact on the level of applications: indeed, numbers continued to rise after 1988, reaching 44,840 in 1991; and after a fall in 1992–3, they increased again in 1994 and 1995.[9]

The next target of legislation was reception conditions for asylum-seekers. The 1996 Asylum and Immigration Act limited the welfare benefits for asylum-seekers awaiting an appeal decision and, controversially, withdrew benefits from those who claimed asylum in-country, as opposed to when they arrived at the port of entry. It also established a 'white list' of safe countries where there was considered to be no serious risk of persecution and further tightened provisions for appealing against rejected claims. The Labour administrations of 1997 onwards largely built on this approach. The 1999 Asylum and Immigration Act targeted reception conditions, replacing cash benefits with a controversial voucher system and making support for accommodation conditional on participation in a dispersal scheme.

Interestingly, it was the provisions on welfare support that prompted the most criticism from opposition parties, NGOs and some sections of the general public. There was far more resistance to the notion of reduced welfare support, vouchers and dispersal than to provisions on refugee recognition as such. This was in contrast to the German debate, where the most sensitive areas of reform pertained to the issue of the right to asylum rather than to social conditions for applicants. This reflected in part the different configuration of legal constraints to asylum legislation in the two countries. The UK lacks robust constitutional and judicial checks on state discretion over legal procedures for assessing asylum applications or for defining refugee status. Germany, by contrast, has been more cautious about eroding its constitutionally embedded humanitarian commitment to accept refugees. The divergence is also a function of the persisting British pre-occupation with race relations. One of the concerns voiced about the 1996 and 1999 acts was that their provisions would create a two-tier welfare system, stigmatizing asylum-seekers and thereby potentially damaging race relations.[10] The implication was that measures discriminating against asylum-seekers could be interpreted as a form of racial discrimination and thus risked being socially divisive. Such concerns are far less prominent in the German debate.

Nonetheless, the British preoccupation with race relations has made asylum-seekers a relatively easier target for restriction than other categories of immigrants. Politicians from all parties have tended to justify more restrictive measures in terms of limiting *abuse* of the welfare and asylum systems. Such abuse is portrayed as imposing a burden on British people of all ethnic groups, as well as on genuine refugees. Thus in the parliamentary debates over the 1996 and 1999 bills, many MPs were keen to stress that the issue was not about race, but rather about limiting abuse by 'bogus' asylum-seekers, who were, as one Conservative MP put it, 'the enemy of hard-working people in this country of all races'.[11] The emphasis was picked up by the popular media, which published endless stories about fraud or abuse but, by and large, avoided overtly racist or discriminatory rhetoric. This is not to deny that there was a strong element of racial discrimination influencing asylum policy or that far-right parties such as the British National Party did not use more racist arguments to oppose immigration and asylum. Rather, the point is that such argumentation has been rendered less and less acceptable in mainstream public debate, with even the Conservative Party keen to portray itself as supporting and representing a multicultural society. It was far safer to steer clear of race issues and focus instead on problems of control and abuse.

## Italy: towards convergence with other EU states

There has been far less debate on the problem of asylum abuse in Italy. There are few legal or economic advantages to lodging an application for asylum, and most immigrants choose to reside and work illegally rather than to acquire the status of asylum-seeker. Indeed, until 1990 Italy's asylum law was virtually non-existent. The 1947 Italian Constitution did grant a right to asylum, but there was no legislation elaborating the rights of asylum-seekers, and those granted refugee status under the constitution had no formal authorization to stay, or any other rights other than that of *non-refoulement*. In this sense, Italy followed the opposite course to the UK and Germany in the 1990s, starting with minimal asylum rights, which were gradually expanded to conform to west European standards.

The Martelli Law of 1990 was the first attempt to rectify the gaps in Italy's asylum policy. It dealt with procedures for assessing asylum applications and with reception conditions for asylum-seekers. The law dropped Italy's hitherto geographical restriction on asylum, which had limited the status of refugee to those from Europe. But given the low number of asylum-seekers in Italy, the law and the decrees subsequently implementing it were surprisingly strict. Asylum-seekers with no other form of support were permitted to apply for assistance from the local police headquarters (*questura*), but support was restricted to a maximum of 45 days. Asylum-seekers were also prohibited from working. In fact, most assistance for asylum-seekers was organized by local municipalities or NGOs or, since 2001, through a scheme called the National Asylum Programme, financed by the European Union.[12] In the absence of a more comprehensive support system, many asylum-seekers set up makeshift camps at the edges of Italian cities or found jobs on the black market.

The 1990 rules on access to the asylum process were also restrictive, allowing Italy to reject asylum-seekers at the border if they had arrived via third countries which were signatories to the Geneva Convention and had spent some time in them. This represented a far more stringent requirement than the concept of 'safe third countries' being implemented in most other west European states. Interestingly, the number of asylum-seekers did rise to a peak of 23,300 in 1991, but subsequently it fell back to around 1,500 to 2,500 per year until 1997, when it rose to 11,000. But even at the 1991 peak, the number involved was minimal by comparison with the level of illegal migrants.

In this sense, one may well be tempted to ask why the centrist government of 1990 introduced such stringent rules. As we have seen, this was a period in which migration issues in general were becoming increasingly politicized. Moreover, Italy was under pressure from other EU states and its future Schengen partners to restrict illegal flows. Under these circumstances, it would have been politically difficult for the government to introduce a more substantial liberalization of asylum rules.

Italy did, however, offer other forms of protection over this period. The categories of humanitarian status and temporary protection were developed in order to respond to larger numbers of refugees from the former Yugoslavia, Somalia, Albania and Kosovo. The 1996 centre-left Ulivo coalition also attempted to develop asylum provisions further. In 1998 a more elaborate law on asylum and humanitarian protection aimed to define asylum procedures more clearly and to provide better guidance to municipalities on registration and social assistance for asylum-seekers.[13] The law was approved by the Senate but was not adopted by the Chamber of Deputies. Since then, asylum provisions have been further restricted by the 2002 Bossi-Fini Law (see Chapter 2). This law expanded the possibilities for the detention of asylum-seekers who had entered illegally and introduced accelerated procedures for examining their asylum applications. It was therefore clearly targeted against illegal entrants, again demonstrating how the Italian preoccupation with problems of migration control has spilled over to the treatment of other categories of migrants.

## ILLEGAL IMMIGRATION AS A SECURITY THREAT

As many authors have pointed out, the phenomenon of illegal immigration is almost by definition a product of laws restricting legal routes for migration or asylum.[14] Thus in an important sense it is a problem that has been created by the closure of legal migration and asylum channels from the early 1980s onwards. As in the case of the asylum issue, public concern about illegal migration partly reflects a real rise in the problem, especially since the early 1990s. However, it also suggests a strong symbolic use of the issue, as a strategy for mobilizing electoral support: it has provided a vehicle for exploiting anxieties about security and identity, concerns whose sources are largely unrelated to changes in migration flows as such.

## The rise of illegal migration and migrant-smuggling

Illegal migration was already emerging as a problem in a number of west European states by the early 1980s. France, Belgium, Italy and Spain were among the countries particularly affected by the phenomenon. One reason for this was the relatively good prospects for employment on the black market in some of these countries and/or a lack of strict internal checks. The choice of these countries also reflected the role of migration networks – contacts between newly arriving migrants and their family and friends already resident in these states, who could provide financial assistance for travel or help with accommodation and work. This made it relatively easy to reside and work in the European Community without a permit, and in many cases made the irregular route more attractive than the asylum system. These countries also had periodic regularization programmes or amnesties, which allowed illegal residents to legalize their status and almost certainly acted as a 'pull' factor for would-be migrants.

By the end of the 1980s the problem of illegal migration was beginning to affect all EC states. This was in large part a consequence of new legislation on migration and asylum (see above). Restrictive provisions on entry and asylum made it increasingly difficult for migrants to find legal routes into European states. Tighter visa requirements, carrier sanctions, readmission agreements, accelerated asylum procedures and 'white lists' of safe countries made it almost impossible for either refugees or economic migrants to enter legally. Meanwhile, the removal of emigration restrictions in former communist countries increased the possibilities for illegal entry via land borders with Germany, Austria and Italy, as well as via the Adriatic into Italy. This facilitated illegal flows of nationals from central and eastern Europe and the western Balkans and also transit migration via these countries from the former Soviet countries, the Middle East, Asia and even Africa. Finally, the elimination of internal borders between EU states made illegal migration at external borders a subject of concern for all member states, particularly those in the Schengen area. Those entering via the more porous coastal borders of Greece, Italy and Spain could move on to other EU states with relative ease, prompting EU calls for states at the edges of Europe to tighten their border controls.

Yet paradoxically, strengthened border controls from the early 1990s onwards in some ways exacerbated the problem, driving many potential migrants to seek the assistance of organized migrant-smugglers or -traffickers.[15] This development may not in itself have increased the level of illegal migration (although this is difficult to ascertain), but it has increased the dangers linked to illegal entry. Images of people arriving hidden in container ships, lorries or fishing boats became a focus of media attention, and heightened the sense that European states were unable to control the problem. Illegal migration has often also been accompanied by the exploitation of those being smuggled, thus giving rise to the phenomenon of people-trafficking – the employment of illegal immigrants as irregular (and sometimes forced) labour in sweatshops, farms, catering or prostitution. The people-trafficking industry worldwide was estimated to be worth around $7 billion in 1997, with figures suggesting that around 400,000 people are trafficked into Europe every year.[16]

## Divergent reactions in European states

Despite a number of common European and international efforts to combat the problem (discussed in Chapter 5) the debate on illegal migration and national responses to the problem have taken divergent forms in different EU states. Germany and Italy both have relatively porous borders, with Germany sharing a 1,744-km land border with Poland and the Czech Republic and with Italy struggling to manage a 7,600-km coastline, parts of which are accessible from Tunisia, Albania and Turkey. However, while the German debate has tended to focus on the problem of irregular employment, the Italian debate has been preoccupied with illegal entry and criminality.

Italy first experienced significant flows from 1984 onwards, with an estimated 300,000–350,000 entering or overstaying between 1984 and 1989.[17] Conflict in the former Yugoslavia and the crisis in Albania in the early 1990s triggered an additional influx, with large numbers of refugees and migrants arriving illegally by boat. In addition, illegal immigrants from China, Bangladesh, the Philippines, Turkey and Iraq have been using Tunisia, Greece, Albania and Turkey as transit countries to travel into Italy. Between July 1997 and January 1998 alone, an estimated 3,000 Kurds from northern Iraq and Turkey were smuggled to Italy by boat.[18] The total number of people illegally entering in 2001 was estimated by the Interior Ministry at 20,000. Many of these stayed in Italy, where there were good possibilities for irregular employment, especially in the industrialized north. Others travelled on to other European countries, including France, Germany and the UK.

It was precisely this problem of transit to other countries that prompted concerns among EU countries about Italy's membership of the Schengen

Agreement, and its participation was therefore delayed until 1997.[19] Calls for better management of Italy's borders have placed considerable pressure on both centre-left and right-wing governments to step up controls on illegal immigration. However, increasing anxiety over the security impact of illegal migration originated above all from internal political dynamics. As noted in Chapter 2, the collapse of Italy's mainstream political parties in 1992 created opportunities for the growth of new and often populist political forces keen to exploit migration issues. The Lega Nord, Alleanza Nazionale and subsequently Forza Italia all mobilized support through linking illegal immigration to problems of criminality and internal security.

Since the early 1990s, border controls have been stepped up, with the Guardia di Finanza, or customs guard, redeployed from monitoring land borders to patrolling the coast. A series of decrees and laws in the second half of the 1990s aimed to facilitate the expulsion of illegal immigrants, especially those involved in crime. The Dini Decree of 1995 restricted the right of appeal for those receiving expulsion orders, and the 1998 Single Act allowed the detention of undocumented migrants for up to 30 days. In March 2002 Silvio Berlusconi announced a state of emergency following the arrival in Sicily of a ship carrying 928 illegal immigrants, mostly Kurds, and he granted special powers to the police to expedite expulsion procedures.

Harsh measures on illegal entry contrast with the relatively lax approach to addressing irregular employment, which is almost certainly a central factor attracting illegal migrants to Italy. Interestingly, Italy also continued with the policy of regularization of illegal immigrants over the same period, with new programmes in 1997, 1998 and 2000 carried out under centre-left governments. The result is a seemingly paradoxical combination of stringent measures to control entry and almost no attempt to address migration 'pull' factors. It implies a highly selective channelling of the migration problem onto border control and criminality, with a simultaneous toleration of an economically beneficial irregular labour force.

By contrast, the debate on illegal migration in Germany has tended to focus on the problem of illegal employment. The problem of illegal entry was a prominent issue after 1989, but a series of readmission agreements with central and east European countries, coupled with intensive efforts to strengthen border controls, appear to have limited the level of illegal entry. Official figures show that the number of illegal border crossings diminished from around 55,000 in 1993 to 20,000 in 1997. Most of the apprehensions were of nationals from Romania, Albania and Bulgaria. However, figures suggesting a decrease in border apprehensions do not take into account the problem of the illegal residence and employment of those entering on tourist visas. Since 1991, nationals from Hungary, Poland, the Czech Republic and

Slovakia have been entitled to three-month tourist visas for Schengen countries. Many take on illegal employment during this period or overstay their visas and reside illegally in Germany. This potential for overstay, together with the ongoing problem of illegal entry, has raised concerns about native workers being undercut by cheap, illegal labour, most notably in the construction industry.

The Kohl administration began to draw attention to linkages between unemployment and illegal labour in the run-up to the September 1998 elections. The government introduced a number of measures to crack down on illegal employment, which it claimed was preventing some of Germany's four million unemployed from finding work. This represented a strategic shift from a focus on asylum questions to the issue of illegal migration – a good example of the way in which German party politics has instrumentalized migration issues.[20] The incoming SPD–Green government of 1998 downplayed the importance of illegal immigration, however, and helped to focus the debate on the problem of how best to regulate flows rather than on how to keep immigration to zero. The CDU–CSU have more or less taken up this agenda, switching the focus of their programme to questions of citizenship and integration (see Chapter 4). Thus although illegal flows continue, they have not been a major focus of the debate on immigration since 1998.

In the UK, by contrast, the problem of illegal entry has become a highly sensitive issue despite relatively low numbers of illegal entrants. The UK famously has a tradition of relying on borders as its primary form of migration control. This is for obvious geographical reasons as well as because of a reluctance to introduce systematic internal controls on residents. Border controls have by and large been effective in keeping down the level of illegal entry. In fact, most of those illegally resident in the UK enter on valid visas and simply overstay or fail to respect deportation orders once their asylum applications have been rejected. It is this emphasis on border control that explains the UK's unwillingness to join the Schengen countries in eliminating internal border checks.

However, from around the mid-1990s onwards the number of illegal entrants appeared to be on the rise. The number of apprehensions of illegal migrants entering the UK rose from 3,300 in 1990 to over 47,000 in 2000, implying that it was becoming a major destination for immigrants transiting through other EU states.[21] There is only limited research on why this should be the case.[22] It may well be linked to the introduction of more restrictive legislation in countries such as France and Germany and to a perception of the UK as having looser internal controls – once you have managed to enter the country, it is relatively easy to stay and get a job. It is also almost certainly linked to the wide availability of low-skill jobs on the black market, to language and historical links with former colonies and to the existence of migrant networks.[23] Whatever the reasons, a relatively limited number of border crossings received a high degree of media attention and triggered fears about Britain being 'flooded' or 'swamped' with migrants from the continent.

The issue crystallized around the issue of a Red Cross centre for housing illegal migrants in Sangatte near Calais, many of whose residents attempted to cross to Dover via the Channel Tunnel in 2001–2. The Labour government was quick to respond to these concerns, negotiating the closure of the Sangatte centre with the French government in 2002 and launching a number of highly publicized initiatives to combat trafficking and illegal entry (see Chapter 5). More controversially, it also increased the use of detention centres for asylum-seekers in order to facilitate deportation following a negative decision. Other new measures included introducing stricter carrier sanctions and providing new powers to crack down on irregular employment.[24]

## Patterns of exclusion

Since the 1980s, then, the debate on migration in most west European states has focused to a large extent on how to limit irregular immigrants and asylum-seekers. But negative attitudes towards these groups have not just been a result of changes in the scale or nature of asylum and illegal migration flows. In many ways, asylum-seekers and illegal immigrants have provided an easier target for anti-immigration sentiment than long-term residents. The former groups have limited possibilities to mobilize or to campaign for increased rights, partly because of their irregular or pending legal status in receiving states.

The restrictive treatment of asylum-seekers and illegal immigrants has also been more or less legitimized by widespread perceptions that the majority of claims are not genuine or that asylum-seekers are abusing asylum and welfare systems. Illegal immigrants have meanwhile been connected with anxieties about being 'swamped' or 'invaded', and are often linked to problems of criminality and internal security.

Justifications for cracking down on asylum-seekers and illegal immigrants typically (although not exclusively) invoke welfare protection and security arguments rather than ethnocentric or culture-based ones. This has been most markedly the case in the UK and Germany, where asylum-seekers and illegal immigrants are often contrasted with tax-paying, legal residents, including those from ethnic minority groups. This focus on problems of abuse or criminality has enabled politicians to circumvent arguments based on ethnic or racial discrimination. This has been particularly important in the British debate, where political elites are cautious about discussing immigration and asylum issues in a way that could alienate support from ethnic communities or prove to be socially divisive. Emphasizing the problem of asylum abuse also provided a justification for Germany's retreat from its generous constitutional provisions on asylum.

In Italy the pattern of exclusion is somewhat different: illegal labour is widely tolerated but the illegal entry and stay of immigrants of certain nationalities is portrayed as a threat to security. In many ways, the Italian political system has created more opportunities for this sort of populist rhetoric over the past decade. Italy lacks both a German-style constitutional check on the treatment of immigrants, and a typically British concern about race relations. In a period in which more moderate ideologies on migration issues have been largely discredited, right-wing populist parties have had greater scope for promulgating highly irresponsible rhetoric on migration issues.

## THE IMPACT OF RECENT LABOUR MIGRATION POLICIES

How is the labour migration agenda outlined in Chapter 2 likely to affect the treatment of asylum-seekers and illegal immigrants? As noted earlier, some commentators have suggested it could lead to a general liberalization of treatment for all categories, in a quasi-return to the pre-1970s era of labour migration. This was a period in which migration politics were largely clientelist in most states, and there was little public debate on the potential negative repercussions of immigration. Rather, immigration was seen as bringing significant net economic gains. In this context, refugee policy received relatively little attention.

There is little evidence, however, that migration and asylum policy-making can or will revert to this earlier model. Even if some aspects of labour migration policy become clientelist, the treatment of other groups, especially asylum-seekers and illegal immigrants, shows every sign of remaining highly politicized. After all, the factors that originally led to the politicization of migration have not gone away. Electorates are still anxious about socio-economic security, the changing role of the state and declining collective identities; political parties still have strong incentives to compete for their support; and there appears to be a seemingly steady or even growing supply of refugees and would-be migrants.

This suggests that even if some countries are able to secure consensus among mainstream political parties and social partners for new labour migration policies, this consensus is unlikely to extend to all categories of immigration. The temptation for political parties to mobilize public fears about migration will be as strong as ever, and unwanted new entrants, that is asylum-seekers and illegal immigrants, may well be targeted more than ever. Thus rather than introducing more liberal policies towards these categories, west European states may well seek to reinforce the distinction between economically beneficial legal labour migration and forms of unwanted immigration which are associated with criminality, welfare abuse and insecurity.

As yet, it is difficult to ascertain how far this will be the case, as labour migration reforms are relatively new. Nevertheless, it is worth looking at public discourse and legislation on this in Germany and the UK over the past two years in order to see how the two agendas – liberal labour migration on the one hand, and treatment of asylum-seekers and illegal immigrants on the other – are linked. These patterns can then be contrasted with public discourse in Italy, where the government does not appear to have an interest in clarifying the distinction between beneficial migration and unwanted immigration.

## Germany: separate routes for 'humanitarian' and 'economic' categories

The debate on the new migration law in Germany offers a good example of these tendencies. Public discussion of the new provisions on labour migration has echoes of the economic arguments about the benefits of migration prevalent in the 1950s and 1960s. Schröder has justified the new measures as essential for German competitiveness and economic modernization. The new policies have also had the backing of employers and unions, the client partners in the formation of migration policy in the guest-worker era. One might therefore expect these positive economic arguments to be carried over to other categories of immigrants – asylum-seekers and illegal immigrants.

However, politicians of all parties have been keen to keep the two issues separate, albeit for different reasons. In the report of the cross-party Süssmuth Commission, which was highly influential in shaping the subsequent immigration legislation, asylum-seekers and refugees were dealt with under a section on 'Taking a Humanitarian Approach'; labour migration was dealt with under a section on 'Securing Long-term Prosperity'. Nowhere in the section on a humanitarian approach is there any mention of the possibility that asylum-seekers, those under temporary protection or illegal immigrants might be a source of recruitment for labour migrants. Indeed, the section on labour migration explicitly precludes the possibility of asylum-seekers in Germany applying for a permit via the proposed points system. Instead, they must leave the country voluntarily and apply for a permit from the outside. This is to 'avoid the pull-effect within the asylum procedure', by 'stating clearly that there is no link between immigration that is granted on humanitarian grounds and labour market-oriented immigration'.[25] It also recommended that the existing one-year ban on work for asylum-seekers should be retained, again to prevent any pull-effects.[26]

The draft immigration bill presented by Interior Minister Otto Schily in August 2001 in many ways went further in its separation of the humanitarian and economic categories. It restricted the right to employment for a number of groups in the humanitarian category which had been granted access to the labour market by previous rules. Those groups granted a residence permit because they could not be deported for humanitarian reasons would no longer automatically receive a work permit. Instead, they would have to wait a year before entering the labour market, as was already the case for asylum-seekers.[27]

The draft also contained more general measures to prevent the abuse of asylum systems. These included the acceleration of asylum procedures (the target for examining applicants would be one year); the restriction of social benefits after three years for certain categories of asylum-seekers whose cases were still being examined; a restriction on the right of children of asylum-seekers to join their parents in Germany if they are older than 12; and renewed emphasis on enforcing the return of rejected applicants. The original proposals from the Interior Ministry also rejected a number of the more liberal proposals of the Süssmuth Commission, such as the extension of the definition of 'refugee' to include gender-based persecution and persecution by non-state actors. One exception to this general restriction of asylum provisions was the status of those granted Geneva Convention refugee status, who were now eligible for a permanent residence permit after three years (previously it had been eight), thus bringing their position into line with those granted refugee status under the Basic Law.[28]

At the same time, the government was under pressure from its Green Party coalition partner to liberalize some of the provisions. On 3 September 2001 the Greens adopted a conclusion at their party conference rejecting the bill on the grounds that it would lead to a 'significant deterioration for both migrant residents and refugees'.[29] In subsequent discussions in the cabinet, some of the more restrictive provisions were amended. The bill that was finally accepted by the coalition in November 2001 raised the maximum age for children to join their parents in Germany from 12 to 14, and the definition of 'refugee' was extended to include gender-based persecution and persecution by non-state actors.[30]

Despite this pressure from its Green partners, the government, and especially Schily, was keen to emphasize the restrictive aspects of the bill – partly to make it more palatable to the public and to its critics in the CDU and the CSU. The more generous provisions on labour migration were consistently mentioned in the same breath as measures to restrict asylum abuse.[31] Indeed, the government was right to be concerned about criticisms that the legislation was not restrictive enough. When the bill was presented to the Bundestag in December 2001 the CDU–CSU raised 79 objections, many of which covered provisions on asylum. They argued that the law was not tough enough on issues of family reunion and social benefits. Further problems came with the reading of the bill in the Bundesrat, where the government had no firm majority. This time, criticism came not just from the conservative opposition but also from a number of SPD-governed *Länder,* which were concerned about possible additional costs imposed by the legislation.[32] The bill that was voted on in the Bundesrat on 22 March 2002 managed to retain the broader definition of refugee, but the maximum age at which children were entitled to join their parents was reduced again to 12 years.[33]

The debate on the new labour migration provisions thus showed no signs of ushering in more liberal asylum policies. On the contrary, from the outset the issue of the rights and status of asylum-seekers and others in need of protection was kept quite separate from policy towards labour migrants. Both the Süssmuth Commission and the SPD–Green government were careful to ensure that the recruitment of labour migration would be managed through a controlled selection procedure which would not provide a 'pull' factor for illegal immigrants and asylum-seekers. From the outset the bill was restrictive *vis-à-vis* asylum-seekers, at a time when the number of applications in Germany was actually falling.

These observations lend credence to the thesis that the liberalization of immigration policy in fact encouraged a simultaneous tightening of asylum rules – to send out a clear message both to the German public and to potential illegal immigrants and asylum-seekers that Germany was not becoming a 'soft touch' for immigrants. CDU–CSU opposition to the measures was clearly a key contributor to this dynamic, as it put the government on the defensive, making it keen not to be depicted as overly lax on asylum. The government's lack of a clear majority in the Bundesrat and its eagerness to push the bill through both houses before the autumn 2002 election made it more flexible in the face of CDU–CSU demands, with the end result being more restrictive provisions on asylum-seekers.

## The UK: restriction of asylum as a corollary of labour migration reforms

The British case suggests an even stronger tendency to play off the asylum issue against the new migration policy. The way in which the new labour migration rules were presented, and the simultaneous crack-down on illegal migration and asylum-seekers, implied a deliberate packaging of the tougher measures with more liberal migration provisions.

In one sense it is surprising that the Labour government felt the need to present its policy in this manner. After all, in many ways it faced far less of a challenge in generating support for the new labour migration rules than did the German government. The UK enjoyed almost full employment, and there was no significant parliamentary opposition to the government's labour migration reforms. Moreover, the country had no real history of labour recruitment, and thus no collective memory of the unintended consequences of an economically driven immigration policy, as in the German case.

However, we should also recall that the changes were being introduced at a time of rising numbers of asylum-seekers, public anxiety about illegal entry and widespread perceptions of the UK being a 'soft touch' for immigrants and unable to control influx. Moreover, the new legislation was being debated in the immediate aftermath of a right-wing populist electoral breakthrough in France and the Netherlands, which raised cross-party fears about the consequences of failing to address public concerns about immigration.[34] In this context, the Labour government clearly did not want to risk accusations that it was simply opening the gates to further (legal) migration without controlling unwanted influx.

As in Germany, there was no question that labour migrants would be drawn from the pool of asylum-seekers and illegal immigrants. Restrictions on asylum-seekers' access to the labour market remained in place, despite the shortage of workers in many sectors and protests from some backbench MPs and NGOs. The Home Secretary, David Blunkett, was also keen to stress that the new rules for labour migrants would not in any way provide a route for illegal migrants to regularize their status. As articulated in the White Paper, 'Secure Borders, Safe Havens: Integration with Diversity in Modern Britain', the perceived challenge for British immigration policy was, 'How can we open opportunities that allow people who want to work here, and can contribute to our society, to do so without attempting to enter using illegal routes?'[35] This implied a need to prevent the labour migration system 'from being undermined by people coming illegally to the UK or working here in breach of the law'. Again, the message was clear: 'If people want to come to the UK for economic reasons they must apply under the economic routes available to them.'[36]

In fact, as mentioned earlier, on occasions Blunkett presented the new labour migration rules as a part of a strategy for cracking down on illegal immigration. Expanding legal routes was 'an essential part of a concerted drive against illegal immigration' and would 'be a body blow to the gang-masters and people traffickers who bring people to this country illegally'.[37] This notion of labour migration as a means of reducing illegal migration was one part of a wider strategy to combat illegal migration, as presented in the

White Paper and subsequently incorporated into the bill of spring 2002. What the Home Office described as its 'tough new legislation' introduced a raft of measures to restrict illegal entry, residence and employment.[38] It established new powers for searching businesses for illegal immigrants and obliged employers and banks to pass information about suspected illegal entrants on to the Home Office. The penalty for migrant-smuggling was increased to 14 years, while provisions on carrier sanctions were made tougher – carriers would in future need to obtain clearance for passengers, the 'Authority to Carry' scheme.

The legislation also contained stringent measures on asylum-seekers. It introduced a new system of accommodation centres for asylum-seekers and a highly controversial provision on the teaching of asylum-seekers' children within these centres rather than in the normal school system. The provision of welfare support to asylum-seekers was made conditional on regular reporting to special reporting centres. The legislation also established special 'removal centres' where rejected asylum-seekers could be detained pending their deportation. Moreover, it sought to prevent abuse of the appeal system, narrowing the grounds on which rejected asylum applicants could appeal against negative decisions. Finally, the legislation made it possible for those convicted of a serious criminal offence to be excluded from refugee status.

The bill's restrictive measures on asylum and illegal immigration received far more attention than the expansion of possibilities for legal labour migration. Blunkett made a point of emphasizing how tough the new asylum measures were, boasting in parliament of one of the new measures that it represented 'one of the toughest yardsticks … in the developed world'.[39] This type of rhetoric and the harsh new provisions on asylum-seekers left little leeway for Conservative criticism. Most of the controversy over the bill revolved around objections from the centre-left that the measures were too restrictive, and there was substantial opposition from the Liberal Democrats and a number of Labour backbenchers. These critics were greatly concerned about the provisions on asylum, especially the possibility of segregated schooling for asylum-seekers' children. Once again, British concern over discrimination and race relations appeared to outweigh issues of refugee protection, as in the case of the new restrictions on the right of asylum-seekers to appeal against a negative decision.[40]

Of course, these restrictive measures should not be understood simply as a means of diverting attention from potentially unpopular labour migration policies. The Labour government was generally keen to demonstrate its readiness to take a tough stance on asylum and illegal immigration, especially at a time of rising support for anti-immigrant populist parties in Europe. This restrictionist agenda would doubtless have been present whether or not the government was concerned about pushing through its more liberal provisions on labour migration. Yet the way in which expanded labour migration provisions were packaged alongside restrictive measures on illegal immigration, and even presented as a means of reducing illegal flows, seemed to indicate a change in the pattern of justification for migration policy. After two decades of unsuccessful attempts to impede almost all categories of economic migration, the government appeared to be willing to make a strong case for welcoming certain types of newcomers, especially economically beneficial labour migrants. This did not emanate from international political pressures or relations with Commonwealth countries, as in the post-Second World War era. Rather, it was a clear response to economic interests. But as a corollary of this new (albeit limited) openness, the government was more determined than ever to combat all forms of illegal entry, employment and asylum abuse. This represented a subtle but important shift in its concept of migration management. The emerging concept recognized the legitimate claims of legal labour migrants, but it was less tolerant than before towards irregular newcomers and those abusing asylum systems.

## Italy: across-the-board restriction

Once again, Italy appears to display a rather different dynamic, with little indication of playing off the restriction of 'unwanted' migrants against the liberalization of economically beneficial labour migration. In fact, the distinction between illegal migrants and regular labour migrants tends to be blurred in public debates. This may seem paradoxical given the public's preoccupation with problems of security, criminality and control linked to illegal migration, which might imply a readiness to distinguish between problematic illegal immigrants and economically beneficial legal labour migrants. Instead, Italy has followed a rather curious path of legislation designed to restrict both legal and illegal immigration and, simultaneously, to continue the regularization of illegal immigrants which will, if anything, encourage more illegal entry.

One of the explanations for this unusual approach lies in Italy's now well-established pattern of recruiting labour migrants from the pool of illegal immigrants already resident in the country. Through a combination of mismanagement and political inertia, Italy has not pursued the type of dual policy approach characteristic of Germany and the UK – that is, attempts to restrict illegal migration while recruiting regular labour migrants through separate, managed channels. Instead, illegal immigrants have become the main source of Italy's much-needed foreign labour, a pattern which has been clearly reinforced by the practice of regularizing illegal immigrants. This has consolidated the notion, held by employers as well as by migrants themselves, that illegal entry and stay is the simplest route to employment and eventually to legal residence status. Illegal migration and regular labour migration are therefore seen more as being on a continuum than as fundamentally separate types of immigration. Many business and employers' groups appear to have little interest in reversing the continuum model; they are content to recruit employees already in Italy and then to ensure that their position is regularized.

A second important reason for this conflation of different categories derives from Italian party political dynamics over the past decade. As noted in Chapter 2, immigration has been one of the central campaigning issues for parties within the right-wing Casa delle Libertà coalition. Despite Berlusconi's pro-business leanings, he has been cautious about pursuing an economically oriented labour migration policy. Instead, the government has treated both illegal immigration and labour migration as problematic and has passed legislation designed to restrict the levels of both. As also noted in Chapter 2, the presence of Bossi and his more radical right Lega Nord in the government has undoubtedly fuelled this across-the-board restrictive agenda. The Lega Nord is keen to assert a more independent political profile by positioning itself to the right of its coalition partners on questions of immigration. This in turn exerts pressure on the other partners to demonstrate their willingness to be tough on migration. The competition between Casa delle Libertà parties to prove their restrictive credentials has filtered through to the rhetoric and legislation on legal labour migration.

# 4

## *Labour migration, integration and diversity*

The new debate on labour migration has not only raised questions about how many or what sorts of newcomers to admit into western Europe. It has also brought to the fore problems of the integration of long-term residents or ethnic minority groups. The concern here is not so much one of managing migration flows, but rather that of how best to ensure the socio-economic and political incorporation of immigrants into receiving societies. The success or failure of incorporation has implications both for the well-being of immigrants and minority groups themselves and for many aspects of the social, economic and cultural life of the receiving country. Concerns about the impact of 'failed integration' on receiving societies have been articulated as worries about social tensions in inner cities, rising criminality, declining educational standards, rising welfare costs or the dilution of the traditional values or identity of the receiving society.

Whether or not these problems are in fact caused by the presence of immigrants and ethnic minorities, the perceived linkages between immigrant integration and broader socio-economic problems need to be taken seriously. They are likely to feed anxieties about the potential impact of further labour immigration. If we have failed to integrate those who have been living here for several decades or second- and third- generation immigrants, so the argument runs, then what hope do we have of integrating large numbers of additional labour immigrants in the coming years? Such worries have been voiced notably by opponents of increased labour migration in Germany, where the CDU and CSU have argued that it would be unwise to admit more immigrants before those already resident have been effectively integrated. In Italy, concerns about the cultural compatibility of non-European immigrants, and especially Muslims, are consistently marshalled as a central argument against immigration. The UK has also recently had a debate on integration and citizenship, although these have not been explicitly linked as yet to the challenge of incorporating additional labour migrants.

The debate on integration will therefore clearly affect the emerging labour migration agenda. Concerns about failed integration are likely to come increasingly to the fore in the context of plans to increase immigrant intake, and will almost certainly be mobilized by anti-immigration political groups in order to oppose plans for reforming labour migration policies. This raises a number of central issues for future approaches to integration in Europe. Why do integration strategies appear to have had such limited success in many cases? What is the source of public concern about integration and how far is it grounded in fact? And does the challenge of integration cast doubt on the feasibility or desirability of the new labour migration agenda?

This chapter starts by considering what west European societies mean by, or expect of, immigrant integration and how they have attempted to promote this. It then considers why the question has become so fraught over the past few years. Finally, it examines how the debate on so-called 'failed integration' relates to the new labour migration agenda. Is there a likelihood that concerns about integration will frustrate liberalizing tendencies, or might they instead trigger a rethink of integration policies?

## CONCEPTS OF INTEGRATION

The concept of integration in its broadest sense implies a process of incorporating immigrants and ethnic minorities into the economy, society and political life of their host country. The economic and social dimensions of integration are probably the least difficult to define, implying, at a minimum, insertion into the labour market and education and welfare systems. Cultural integration is less easy to pin down, but is usually taken to involve knowledge of the host country's language, some understanding of its society and respect for its basic norms. Finally, political integration implies the right to vote and to stand for election, usually acquired through naturalization. In many countries it is understood as the final stage of a successful process of integration.

Beyond this general concept, there are significant national and ideological variations as to how far immigrants are expected to adapt to the receiving society's culture and values and to participate in its social and political life. Here it is useful to introduce a distinction (albeit a simplified one) between two dominant concepts of integration. First is the concept of multiculturalism, which sets lower expectations about the degree to which immigrants should adapt to their receiving societies. The multicultural concept allows space for the coexistence of groups with diverse culture, norms and even language. The rationale may be pragmatic, insofar as it is considered unfeasible or counterproductive to put pressure on immigrants to give up their own identities. Or it may be defended out of a more normative commitment to the value of cultural pluralism, which sees diversity as intrinsically desirable. The second is the concept of assimilation, which expects immigrants – or at least their children – to assume the values, characteristics and behaviour of members of the receiving society. The assimilationist concept typically goes hand in hand with a stronger conception of what it means to be a member of society or a citizen. These two concepts are useful for identifying different philosophies and goals of integration. In practice, however, most west European governments have opted for something between the two poles.

The multicultural concept is typically associated with the Anglo-Saxon model of a liberal pluralist state, which values the individual freedom of its members, allows scope for a considerable degree of cultural diversity and embraces only a minimal concept of shared identity or 'overlapping consensus' between residents.[1] In western Europe, this model is most usually associated with the UK, where (so political philosophers would argue) there is a weak concept of citizenship, based on common adherence to individualist liberal principles. Arguably, this liberal pluralist model also assumes a more limited role for the state in redressing socio-economic inequalities between different groups, implying a higher tolerance of disparities in wealth between different classes or ethnic groups.[2] The more demanding concept of assimilation, by contrast, is premised on a more elaborate concept of what is expected of membership or citizenship. This 'thicker' concept may be expressed as a French-style republican commitment to the civic participation of *citoyens*, or it may be derived from a more ethnocentric concept of a shared national or cultural identity. Either way, full incorporation may not be achieved until immigrants are willing and able to conform to a more detailed set of conditions for membership.

The different conceptions of integration are closely linked to the way different states conceive their own national identity and what it means to be a member. These traditions of thought on nationality have been shaped in different European states through experiences of nation-building, international and civil conflict, and democratization.[3] However, they should not be seen as unified or fixed. One can discern multiple traditions of thought on citizenship and national identity within most states, and it is not always a foregone conclusion which concept will come to dominate policy when states are confronted with new immigration challenges. Moreover, these philosophies have in turn been influenced by more recent experiences of dealing with immigration since the Second World War, which have forced many European states to re-evaluate and revise traditional notions of citizenship and identity. The fact of immigration, then, can itself shape broader conceptions of membership and national identity.

## The UK: race relations and multiculturalism

In the UK the dominant philosophy of identity and citizenship can be characterized as relatively culturally pluralist, with a rather minimalist liberal conception of citizenship, at least compared to its continental neighbours. Ethnic and cultural pluralism was in part a legacy of the union between England, Wales, Scotland and Ireland, which brought together four distinct national groups under one state structure. It was reinforced by a colonial conception of British 'subjecthood', which defined membership on the basis of territorial residence rather than descent or ethnicity (so-called *jus soli*, as opposed to *jus sanguinis*). As indicated in Chapter 1, this had far-reaching consequences for the treatment of Commonwealth immigrants after the Second World War, with newcomers from former and current colonies automatically entitled to full citizenship. Although citizenship rules have subsequently been revised, Commonwealth nationals resident in Britain are still entitled to vote in national elections.

Also significant in shaping approaches to integration has been Britain's tradition as a liberal pluralist state, which, to simplify somewhat, embraces a philosophy of minimalist state intervention, individual freedom and limited expectations about the duties and shared characteristics of citizens. This implies that even when immigrants have arrived and settled in Britain, there are relatively limited, or at least ill-defined, expectations of what is required of them in order to become full members of society. Thus the UK has had relatively low expectations of what integration should involve. Indeed, the emphasis has been on the far more minimalist goal of preventing an almost Hobbesian scenario of conflict between different groups.[4] The key to achieving peaceful coexistence between ethnic groups is seen to lie in the concept of 'race relations', which focuses on eliminating discriminatory treatment of ethnic groups and creating equal opportunities for immigrants. This concept of 'integration', if it can be regarded as such, is far less elaborate than French or German demands for civic or cultural assimilation.

Although this approach has been influenced by traditions of liberal thought and weak notions of British identity, it has also been a product of far more pragmatic considerations.[5] Since the arrival of the first groups of Caribbean immigrants in 1946, British elites have been preoccupied with concerns about tensions and conflict between 'black' (West Indian or African) immigrants and 'Asian' ones (those from the Indian sub-continent), on the one hand, and the indigenous white British community on the other. This automatic definition of the problem as one of 'race' reflects a distinctively

British colonial conception of ethnic difference.[6] It was also one that permeated popular attitudes in postwar Britain, with black and Asian immigrants finding themselves subject to widespread discrimination on racial grounds.

The question of how best to manage race relations was pushed up the political agenda in 1958, when a series of 'race riots' broke out in Nottingham and parts of London. The general consensus that emerged in the aftermath of the riots was that race relations would best be managed through a combination of restricting further New Commonwealth immigration and legislation to prevent discrimination on racial grounds. Thus consecutive governments gradually limited the citizenship and immigration rights of former colonies (see Chapter 1), while introducing a series of race relations acts. The first of these laws, introduced in 1965, was a somewhat limited set of provisions to outlaw discrimination in 'places of public resort'. It was extended in 1968 to cover housing, employment and treatment by the police, although racial discrimination remained a civil rather than a criminal offence, and the legislation proved difficult to implement in practice.[7] A further act in 1976 focused on access to employment. It also created the independent Commission for Racial Equality, to promote equality of opportunity and combat racial discrimination.

The logic behind the legislation was to pre-empt inter-ethnic tensions, in what has been termed a paternalistic pattern of extending rights 'from above'. This has been contrasted with the pattern of anti-discrimination action in the United States in response to pressure from highly organized and mobilized ethnic groups. In the UK, it was the fear rather than the reality of mobilized group action that motivated the reforms. As Roy Jenkins, Home Secretary in 1965, put it: 'it is far better to put this Bill on the Statute Book now, before social stresses and ill-will have the chance of corrupting and distorting our relationships'.[8] The notion that anti-discrimination measures were the best means of securing this end reflected a more or less explicit assumption that inter-ethnic conflict was caused by lack of equal opportunities for minority groups and that the central task for successful integration lay in eliminating these formal barriers. There was less explicit emphasis on possible socioeconomic sources of these constraints, such as poverty, lack of education, or the concentration of ethnic minorities in particular inner city areas.

At the same time, governments and the courts in the UK have been relatively flexible in allowing minority groups cultural and religious freedoms in public life. This was reflected, for example, in rulings on respect for special religious requirements for dress, diet or prayer in the workplace and schools. From the 1980s onwards, it was also evident in the attempt to promote multicultural values in schools, including legislation allowing for state subsidization of religious schools of all denominations (until then only Christian and Jewish schools had benefited from this provision). Some local authorities with large numbers of ethnic minorities have gone much further in their attempts to represent the interests of ethnic groups. They have established special 'racial equality units', introduced more progressive concepts of multiculturalism in schools and promoted affirmative action for members of minority groups.

To be sure, there have been important counter-tendencies in British thinking on immigrant integration. The racist British National Front, and latterly the British National Party, have had moderate success in local elections since the 1970s, although they have never won a seat at Westminster. There have also been reactionary voices within the Conservative Party – most notoriously Enoch Powell's 1968 'Rivers of Blood' speech, which presented an apocalyptic vision of a country wracked by violent conflict between different ethnic groups. These more exclusionist ideas continue to influence many of the British public, as reflected in the continued high incidence of discrimination against ethnic minorities. But, for mainly prag-matic reasons, British elites have largely converged in accepting a more liberal and inclusive model, and the concept of multiculturalism has achieved a remarkable degree of acceptance. All three major parties are keen to woo ethnic minority voters, with even the more traditionally nationalistic Conservative Party firmly embracing the notion of a multicultural Britain since the 1990s.

## Germany: social citizenship

Germany, by contrast, is often presented as the classic case of a European state attached to an 'ethnic' concept of national identity.[9] There is indeed much to support this view: the project to build a united Germany which emerged in the nineteenth century was to a great extent legitimized by an ethnic conception of the nation, or *Volk*, defined in terms of linguistic and cultural characteristics. This ethnic conception of national membership was in many ways discredited by the experience of the Third Reich, with any hint of expansionist tendencies or notions of ethnic superiority rendered thoroughly taboo. But less compromised elements of the ethnic conception of member-ship nonetheless continued to be influential after the Second World War and to shape responses to immigration. Most obviously, the ethnic concept of identity contributed to an unwillingness to acknowledge that the immigra-tion of guest workers in the 1950s and 1960s could or would result in their permanent residence and integration. The common assumption until the 1980s was that guest workers and their families would not become permanent members of German society. Even once their permanent settlement became an undeniable reality, Germany remained reluctant to allow the naturalization of non-ethnic German immigrants, retaining an essentially *jus sanguinis* conception of nationality.

However, this ethnic conception was certainly not the only tradition of thought influencing approaches to integration. Arguably just as influential was West Germany's commitment to a set of democratic and egalitarian values embodied in both the welfare state system and the German constitution. The welfare state tradition had its sources in pre-First World War and Weimar Germany; after the Second World War it became consolidated through the development of a generous welfare state system. Meanwhile, the postwar constitution earned the status of a quasi-sacred text, enshrining an elaborate system of freedoms and rights. The constitution came to represent a central aspect of West Germany's self-identity, as captured by the notion of 'constitutional patriotism', which many hoped would replace previous ethnocentric based ties of loyalty. Together, these two institutions – the welfare system and the constitution – ensured that although naturalization of immigrants remains the exception rather than the rule until the 1980s, permanent residents were nonetheless entitled to almost all of the generous social rights and benefits accruing to citizens.

This entitlement to socio-economic rights was not taken for granted from the outset. Indeed, the guest workers who arrived in the 1950s and 1960s initially had restricted access to welfare benefits (for example, they did not enjoy access to long-term unemployment or disability benefits), and they had very limited civil and political rights. But from the 1970s onwards, immigrants' rights were extended to incorporate almost all of the rights and benefits enjoyed by German nationals in the spheres of welfare, education, health and employment. As in the UK, there were also a number of programmes to provide special assistance to immigrants, mainly administered through voluntary organizations. Three large charities were responsible for providing advice and social services to immigrants, and by the early 1990s they had established around 600 local foreigners' bureaux.[10] More progressive *Länder* such as Berlin and Hamburg also sponsor migrants' cultural, youth and women's organizations, and the Berlin Senate has established a special Commissioner for Foreigners' Affairs, who proposes measures and coordinates action related to integration.[11] Nonetheless, the main tool of integration was seen as incorporation into the labour market and welfare system. In a booming economy with a highly developed welfare system, this amounted to fairly generous treatment in the 1950s and 1960s. Indeed, many assumed that allowing immigrants equal access to these rights and benefits would ensure full socio-economic integration, rendering targeted programmes superfluous.

A number of commentators have argued that the German approach to integration created a special status of 'denizenship' or 'social citizenship', which fell short of full political citizenship but still implied permanent membership and near-equal status in the host society.[12] Such a concept fits well both with the constitutional and welfare state strands in postwar German political thought and with the country's traditionally ethnocentric conception of membership. It implies that Germany should respect and ensure the welfare of permanent residents, but that as non-ethnic Germans they and their children could not ultimately become full members of the community. Instead, there should be, in Kohl's words, a 'relaxed coexistence between foreigners and Germans'.[13] Paradoxically, the virtues of this form of denizenship were also praised by many on the left. A number of politicians saw it as a means for ethnic minorities to retain their distinct cultural identity while enjoying equal social and economic rights. Some scholars even embraced such a status as an indication of the declining relevance of the nation-state, seeing it as representing a new form of 'postnational member-ship', which removed the significance or urgency of attaining citizenship.[14]

Nevertheless, the importance of 'missing' citizenship became more apparent in the late 1980s and the 1990s as Germany granted almost automatic citizenship rights to hundreds of thousands of *Aussiedler* from central and eastern Europe, 'ethnic Germans' whose ancestors had settled outside Germany generations ago. This possibility was denied to second- and even third-generation immigrants from Turkey born and raised in Germany, an anomaly which became increasingly untenable. Arguably, the ethnic concept also lost force after German reunification in 1990. Unification removed the symbolic importance of retaining an ethnic criterion for justify-ing claims to a unified Germany.[15] Moreover, Germany was clearly out of step with most of its EU neighbours. By the late 1980s, continued adherence to the ethnic concept of citizenship meant that Germany had the lowest naturalization rate in Europe, with less than half a per cent of its immigrant population entitled to become citizens.[16]

From the beginning of the 1990s, a succession of new laws gradually facilitated the naturalization of foreigners. In 1990 the Foreigners Law made naturalization the rule rather than the exception for second- and third-generation immigrants who had been resident in Germany for at least eight years and for first-generation immigrants resident for more than 15 years. Two years later, the famous *Asylkompromiss* between the CDU, the CSU, the FDP and the SPD included an agreement to make naturalization a right rather than a question of state discretion, and to abolish the notion of cultural assimilation as a precondition. Legislation in 1998 loosened restrictions on dual nationality, paving the way for immigrants – notably the Turkish community – to retain the nationality of their country of origin if they became German.

Nevertheless, ethnic minorities in Germany have clearly suffered from their failure to be accepted as full members with equal political and civil rights. Despite expanded opportunities for naturalization, the notion that ethnic minorities can be 'real' Germans has yet to gain widespread acceptance. This is partly a result of (and in turn contributes to) the absence of ethnic minorities in public life, especially in politics and the media. This appears to be gradually changing now. But given the very late recognition of the permanence of immigration and its slowness in introducing more expansive naturalization rules, Germany still has a long way to go before the notion of a multi-ethnic society becomes a normal part of its self-perceived identity.

## Italy: still lacking a concept of integration

In some ways, Italy's approach to integration today is reminiscent of that of guest-worker countries 20 years ago. The country has yet to begin to grapple seriously with the problem of integration, and there remains a widespread, if often implicit, assumption among many of the public and some political elites that immigrants are temporary residents.[17] Moreover, panic over apparently uncontrollable illegal entry has tended to dominate the policy agenda since the early 1990s, leaving little space for reflection on the complex issues raised by integration. As in the German case, it may take some years before Italy comes to terms with the fact of large-scale permanent settlement. Apart from some limited attempts to deal with integration in legislation of 1986, 1992 and 1998, most efforts have been undertaken by trade unions, Catholic organizations and immigrant groups, and there is nothing approaching consensus between political elites on strategies for dealing with integration. For these reasons, it is difficult to forecast what sorts of models or concepts will come to shape Italian approaches to integration.

In terms of conceptions of membership and identity, Italy shares some of the features of the German case. It experienced a relatively late process of nation-building in 1860s, which, as in Germany, attempted to draw on a concept of shared identity. Yet this notion of an Italian identity never had the same force or appeal as the German one, with the Italian population lacking a unified language, culture or sense of loyalty to the central state at the time of Italian unification.[18] The formation of the Italian nation-state was based more on compromise between different regional units than on a transcending idea of a homogeneous Italian political community.[19] Unlike in other European countries, unification was not popularly conceived of as a struggle for national liberation.[20] Loyalties to region and family generally remained more salient than national patriotism. Attempts by the Italian intellectual movement, the Risorgimento, to forge a national myth failed to inspire support for nationalism from either bourgeois or working-class

Italians. Indeed, a strong concept of nationalism only briefly gained credence during the Fascist era, and was subsequently discredited, at least in centre and left-wing circles, after the Second World War.[21] The importance of the Catholic Church further diluted the notion of a homogeneous national community, promoting as it did a cosmopolitan rather than a nationally delimited community of values.

One of the more pronounced cleavages to emerge was a north–south divide, a pattern of discrimination against the underdeveloped south often premised on notions of the ethnic inferiority of southerners. This cleavage resurfaced in the politics of the Lega Nord in the 1990s, most dramatically through its secessionist agenda. Interestingly, this party has also propagated an extreme anti-immigrant line, drawing on notions of cultural and religious differences between (at least north Italian) residents and foreigners. This overlap of regional chauvinism and anti-immigrant discourse suggests that Italian concepts of membership are not straightforwardly nationalistic. Rather, they are just as likely to be rooted in exclusivist notions of regional identity or, increasingly, in European or Christian versus Muslim, Arab or African identity.

Interestingly, though, ethnocentric concepts of membership were conspicuously absent from public discussion on immigration until the early 1990s. Until then, the two major centrist parties, the Democrazia Cristiana and the Partito Socialista Italiano, had dominated these debates, converging on a moderate position which recognized humanitarian duties to newcomers and sought to align Italy's policy to EC standards. The media likewise adopted a moderate and largely sympathetic tone on immigration issues. In any case, immigration was still seen as a transitory problem, not especially affecting Italian society, and as such the question of cultural or ethnic difference as a challenge to identity did not arise. However, the political crisis triggered by the corruption trials of 1992–3 upset this consensus. The crisis seriously discredited the two centrist parties and effectively delegitimized the prevailing values and ideology of the postwar political system. The crisis of public confidence in the system created a context in which a disoriented public was searching for new values and for new concepts of political community.[22] At the same time, the demise of the major postwar parties led to a jostling for power among numerous smaller parties, which were searching for a distinctive and appealing political agenda.

It was under these circumstances that small parties such as the Lega Nord and the Alleanza Nazionale discovered the electoral dividends of anti-immigrant rhetoric. The Lega Nord began to emphasize the difference between (north) Italians and *extracommunitari*, non-EU immigrants, and proposed a raft of highly restrictive measures against illegal immigrants.

Concerns about ethnic differences were subsequently picked up by Forza Italia. Berlusconi campaigned together with the leader of the Lega Nord, Umberto Bossi, on a strongly anti-immigration platform in the spring 2000 election. The two issued a joint document that rejected 'a universal, multiracial society … rooted in the markets' and allied the parties instead to a 'Christian' model of society based on the 'primacy of the nation understood in the romantic sense, as a nucleus and base of values, religion, culture, language, dress and tradition'.[23]

Such exclusionist notions have not always dominated Italian responses to immigrants. Also important in shaping the Italian debate on immigrant integration have been more inclusionist and anti-racist strands of thought, often articulated by civil society groups. One of these is the Catholic universalist ethic of extending charity and hospitality to those in need, which has led many Catholic organizations to become involved in assisting immigrants, and has prompted Church criticism of some of the current government's more restrictive policies. The second is a more left-wing tradition of solidarity with immigrants, manifested in left-wing political parties' traditional defence of immigrant rights and in trade unions' attempts to incorporate legal immigrants (although this is also driven by quite pragmatic considerations). Often these more solidaristic views have been linked with an almost nostalgic view of Italy as a former emigration country, implying a special understanding of immigrants and a duty of reciprocity to those now seeking to settle in Italy. These groups had some success in influencing government policies from the mid-1980s onwards through bodies such as the Comitato per una legge guista, an alliance of trade unions, NGOs and Catholic organizations which was formed to lobby for more inclusive provisions shortly before the adoption of legislation in 1986. The Patto per un Parlamento antirazzista was another example of an alliance of left-wing politicians, church groups and union-sponsored immigrant groups; it put up candidates in the 1992 parliamentary elections.[24]

In fact, there were some attempts to develop integration policies over this period. A 1986 law entitled legal immigrants to equal labour rights, health and social services, education and family reunion, a progressive step but one which essentially only put Italy in line with minimum international standards.[25] The law also made provisions for a consultative committee to the Ministry of Labour and Social Security, which would include representatives from immigrant organizations. This approach was broadened by the 1990 Martelli Law, which extended access to social assistance, and by the 1998 Turco-Napolitano Act, the 'Single Act', which introduced special support for immigrants learning Italian as well as possibilities for children to learn the language of their country of origin at school. It granted full civil rights and most social rights to legal immigrants, who were now entitled to an unrestricted residence permit after five years. It also created a new body, the Council for Immigrants, which was to represent and promote the concerns of immigrants.

Worthy as these attempts were, they remained essentially piecemeal and limited in impact. Some of them have since been withdrawn or reformed by the right-wing coalition government.[26] Meanwhile, provisions on naturalization, a critical component of integration policy, were being made stricter than before. A nationality law of 1992 replaced the 1912 law, requiring non-EU nationals to be resident in Italy for ten years before being entitled to acquire Italian citizenship. Children born in Italy of non-EU parents would meanwhile have the option of acquiring citizenship at the age of 18, but only if they had been continuously resident in Italy since birth. These provisions brought Italian legislation into line with that of the more restrictive EU countries such as Germany, but at a time when those countries were recognizing that strict rules undermined integration and were in the process of liberalizing them.

One reason for the lack of progress on integration policies appears to have been the absence of a robust programme from the centre-left. Immigration policy has become such a politically contested issue that centre-left parties have been reluctant to bring questions of integration onto the political agenda at all. As one centre-left parliamentarian put it during the debate on the nationality law, her party was reluctant to voice stronger opposition to the basically restrictive law because 'the conditions necessary to launch this debate are not currently in place'.[27] Thus in a period of intensive inter-party struggle and a search to establish credibility with voters, even left-of-centre parties have been cautious about championing the rights of immigrants.

What this may reflect is a broader problem with the ideological basis for pro-immigrant political lobbying in Italy. Both Catholic groups and left-wing parties have tended to adopt mainly ethical arguments for assisting immigrants, to the exclusion of more pragmatic concerns. This emphasis on the ethical ideals of solidarity or humanity appears to have had two consequences. The first is to provide a justification for immigration that may be fairly fragile when confronted with concerns about security or cultural identity. The second is that a focus on the duties of charity or solidarity is in many ways too limited: it implies alleviating hardship and suffering among immigrants instead of addressing the longer-term need for effective legal rights and integration. As some critics have argued, this too falls prey to the assumption that immigration is essentially a short-term phenomenon requiring palliative assistance rather than incorporation.[28]

An important exception to this tendency is the trade unions, which have been active in promoting the integration of the immigrant workers they represent, and on very pragmatic grounds. An estimated 67 per cent of legal immigrant workers are affiliated with a union, an exceptionally high level compared to other European countries.[29] The unions have been keen to incorporate immigrants, to regularize their status and to improve their socio-economic conditions, in large part because of their interest in eliminating illegal labour, which can undercut or displace legal employees. The two major Italian unions, the Confederazione Generale Italiana del Lavoro and the Confederazione Italiana Sindacati dei Lavoratori, have immigrants' bureaux at the district, regional and national level, through which they represent immigrants' claims, and lobby local health and education services to provide better access and services for immigrants.[30] These initiatives go some way towards filling a vacuum left by the state's failure to produce a strategy for integration. But clearly they are no substitute for government action; moreover, they are limited to assistance for those whose status has already been regularized.

Italy can thus be characterized as being in a phase of profound political flux, with no settled consensus on concepts of political community, let alone on immigrant integration. Serious attempts to grapple with questions of integration have been impeded by the anti-immigration rhetoric of right-wing populist parties and by the continued preoccupation with what is considered to be the more urgent issue of controlling illegal entry. Nonetheless, more inclusionist strands, whether leftist, trade unionist or Catholic, continue to surface in the debate, even though they are frustrated at present by a lack of robust support from left-wing political parties. Moreover, as an EU member state, Italy will be obliged to incorporate anti-discrimination laws emanating from EU cooperation in this area.[31] As a result, EU cooperation could go some way to help in filling a gap in national-level provisions and shaping a more inclusive agenda.

### PROBLEMS OF 'FAILED INTEGRATION'

Germany and the UK have both been subject to growing doubts about the effectiveness of existing approaches to integration over the past few years. Whereas discussion on integration policy has emerged only very recently in Italy, in both Germany and the UK there has been a growing tendency to question the wisdom of various assumptions which were made about the integration of immigrants from the 1950s onwards. It is worth examining these two cases in more detail.

Doubts about integration have been triggered in part by specific events: riots in the north of England, the terrorist attacks of 11 September 2001 and the ensuing concern about Islamic fundamentalist terrorists in Germany and the UK, and new evidence on the performance of immigrant children in schools. But the prominence of the issue in the media and in political debate also appears to be linked to less tangible anxieties about identity and membership. These concerns have lent a more emotive quality to the debate on integration and citizenship, often obscuring the complexity of the causes of failed integration or exaggerating their impact on host societies.

## Germany: inequality, segregation and cultural difference

In Germany, one of the most prominent issues to emerge since the late 1990s has been that of the apparent obstacles to the integration of second- and third-generation immigrants. The debate has focused predominantly on the Turkish community – the largest ethnic minority group in Germany, and one with disappointing socio-economic indicators. Turkish nationals continue to perform well below average in terms of educational achievement and participation in the labour market. This appears to be partly a result of poor German-language skills. Many Turkish children speak Turkish with their parents and friends, watch Turkish television and attend a Turkish kindergarten; thus they often arrive at German schools with a poor knowledge of German. Linked to this is the issue of accommodation: a large proportion of Turkish immigrants remain concentrated in particular districts of German cities with limited dispersal into other areas. In many cases these communities appear to be trapped in 'ghettoes', with poor housing and high levels of deprivation.[32] Meanwhile, a number of surveys have suggested that there is an increasing tendency among young Turkish immigrants to reject personal identification with German culture and society, as well as declining levels of social interaction with the indigenous German community.[33]

The apparent failure of immigrant integration featured prominently in the German media in 2000–2 and triggered a number of debates on the socio-economic and cultural causes of these problems, and on their repercussions for German society. One set of anxieties revolved around the perceived negative impact of failed integration on the quality of life of indigenous Germans. Concerns were voiced about the welfare costs of supporting high levels of unemployment among the immigrant community, problems of criminality in 'ethnic ghettoes', and fears about the declining quality of education in schools with a high intake of immigrants. Often linked to this were worries about the creation of a permanent underclass of immigrants as in the United States, along with the related problems of ethnic disaffection, criminality and social division. This was often expressed as a fear of multiculturalism, understood as the solidification of ethnic segregation. It was also captured in the notion of 'ethnic mobility traps', which implied that members of immigrant communities might be impeded from moving away from often deprived ethnically concentrated areas, or from gaining higher qualifications or moving to higher-skilled professions than previous generations.[34] These anxieties created a rather bizarre alliance between left-wingers keen to avoid forms of ethnic segregation that would exacerbate or rigidify socio-economic inequalities, and more conservative groups worried about a dilution of German culture through ethnic and cultural pluralism.

The latter concerns came to the fore in the context of a somewhat confused debate on German *Leitkultur* sparked by comments by the president of the CDU–CSU group in the Bundestag, Friedrich Merz. During a debate on new policies on immigration and asylum in October 2000, Merz stated that immigrants should be prepared to commit themselves to German *Leitkultur*, that is a set of basic norms and values including a commitment to the constitution, freedom, individual rights and responsibilities.[35] His comments were rounded on by opposition politicians and immigrant groups. They criticized the notion of a static, homogeneous German culture and the highly assimilationist assumption that immigrants should simply adapt themselves to conform to German values and norms. The CDU quietly shelved the concept, which did not feature in its subsequent party programme.

Nonetheless, the debate did prompt other German political parties to clarify their different lines on what was expected from cultural integration. Interestingly, almost all parties, including the Greens, accept that immigrants should respect a number of basic norms of German society. However, they diverge in terms of how elaborate this list should be. The CDU has dropped the word *Leitkultur* and denies that integration means assimilation, but likewise rejects the concept of multiculturalism. It argues that immigrants should accept the basic values of 'Christian Western culture, which were shaped by Christianity, Judaism, ancient philosophy, humanism, Roman law and the enlightenment'. The CDU's sister party the CSU does use the term *Leitkultur*, which is similarly defined as 'Western European values with roots in Christianity, the enlightenment and humanism'. For the SPD and the Greens, the relevant 'core values' are those set out in the German constitution.[36]

The 2001 report of the cross-party *Zuwanderungskommission* (Immigration Commission) contained a fairly extensive and balanced discussion of the integration problem, and it is worth considering its findings in order to gauge current thinking on the question. The report identified impediments to integration primarily in the weakness of German policies on language, education, housing and naturalization, and proposed a raft of measures to make the process easier, particularly in the area of education and training.

Poor language skills were consistently highlighted as a central problem hindering educational achievement, labour market integration and more extensive contacts with indigenous Germans. The bulk of the recommendations therefore focused on the education and training of immigrant children, and on proposals for integration courses for new immigrants covering language training, an introductory course on Germany's legal and political system and guidance on careers. The report emphasized too the importance of the naturalization of long-term residents and their children and called for more flexibility on rules on dual nationality.

In contrast to the British approach, the report placed far less emphasis on the problem of discrimination. The only proposal on this recommended swift implementation of the EU directives on anti-discrimination, which, as we have seen, EU states were in any case bound to implement by July 2003.[37] Members of the Commission appear to have attributed relatively limited significance to ethnic discrimination as a source of inequality or alienation. Nor was there much in the way of concrete proposals to allow scope for more cultural diversity. In fact, the discussion on immigrant organizations reflected a strong concern that encouraging the 'wrong' sort of ethnic community activities could imply 'a retreat into the immigrant community'. What was advocated instead was a more assimilationist concept of promoting immigrant involvement in German associations.[38] This assimilationist leaning was also illustrated in the discussion of best practice on integration, which focused predominantly on Swedish and Dutch policies in the area of language training.

For all its references to a multi-ethnic society, the report of the *Zuwanderungskommission* implies that the German model of integration stops short of embracing a fully-fledged concept of multiculturalism. The underlying message is that the failure of integration lies primarily in impediments to minorities' learning German and involving themselves in German society, rather than in the failure of German society to adapt its own requirements or expectations of membership. However, the report does imply a more enlightened recognition that the causes of this failure lie at least as much in German policies and attitudes as in the deficiencies of immigrants themselves.

## The UK: beyond the race relations paradigm?

There have also been a number of new developments in debates on integration in the UK. The 1990s saw continued discussion on problems of racial discrimination, sparked by an investigation into the police's handling of a racially motivated murder in London. The Macpherson Report, also referred to as the Stephen Lawrence Inquiry, found evidence of what was termed 'institutional racism' within the police force, prompting the government to introduce new race relations legislation to address forms of direct discrimination in the public services.[39] There was also a renewed debate on multiculturalism, sparked by a Runnymede Trust report which called for a rethink of the concept of 'Britishness', to better incorporate people from different ethnic backgrounds into society.[40] But two new themes also emerged. First, as in Germany, there was growing concern about the problem of integrating second- and third-generation ethnic minorities, a question it had been hoped would be resolved naturally as immigrants' children were raised and educated in Britain. Secondly, and partly linked to the first concern, there was a debate on what was perceived to be the special problem of integrating the Muslim community in Britain.

Regarding the question of second- and third-generation immigrants, Britain has been prey to similar concerns to those in Germany about problems of segregated ethnic communities in inner cities. In the UK Afro-Caribbean and Asian minority groups are highly concentrated in inner city areas of London and the Midlands, which respectively host 45 per cent and 20 per cent of these minorities. Concerns about 'ghettoization', high unemployment and disaffection among these communities are certainly not new, and have repeatedly surfaced after various 'race riots' since 1958. They came to the fore again after a series of riots in a number of northern English towns in summer 2001 involving far-right white youths and members of the Asian community. There followed extensive criticism of local authorities' management of housing, education and social policies in Bradford, Burnley and Oldham which, it was argued, had intensified segregation and divisions between the two communities.[41] But the riots prompted a new debate on the problems of second- and third-generation Asian minorities, especially those from Muslim backgrounds.

Among the causes of the North of England riots, some commentators have highlighted the difficulty faced by young British-born Muslim Asians in identifying either with their parents and religious community or with mainstream British society. One aspect of this was the language and cultural gap between young Muslims and their parents and religious leaders, or Ulema. In Bradford, for example, more than half of the marriages in the Muslim community are still arranged with partners from the Indian subcontinent, who often have limited education and no knowledge of English.[42] Religious leaders are also frequently recruited from South Asia rather than drawn from the expanding pool of graduates from Islamic seminaries in the UK.[43] This creates a cultural rift between many young British Muslims and their parents and Ulema. At the same time, many Asians feel equally distanced from British society, frustrated at continued discrimination and the dearth of good educational and employment opportunities in inner city areas.

Not all interpretations of the problems of British Muslims have been so sympathetic. Since the late 1980s there has also been an increasingly hostile debate on the problem of the Muslim community in Britain, especially in the light of fears about more fundamentalist forms of Islam. This issue first erupted in the context of demonstrations over the Rushdie affair in early 1989, when many British Muslims in Bradford and London demonstrated in favour of the fatwa calling for the execution of the author Salman Rushdie. Although a number of British politicians, and even the Church of England, expressed understanding for the reaction of the Muslim community against the perceived blasphemy in Rushdie's book *The Satanic Verses*, the events highlighted the clash between liberal norms of free speech and some tenets of Islamic law. It prompted the Conservative government to reiterate the importance of all ethnic groups' accepting the principles of freedom of speech and the rule of law. Concerns about Islamic fundamentalism in Britain emerged again in 1991 because of Muslim support for Iraq during the 1991 Gulf War; and, more acutely, a decade later as a result of the 11 September 2001 terrorist attacks in the United States and subsequent media revelations about Al-Qaeda 'sleeper cells' and fundamentalist activities within the British Muslim community.

The Muslim question appeared to be one of the factors prompting the Home Secretary to launch a discussion on British citizenship in 2001. David Blunkett made a number of controversial comments about how effective integration required ethnic minorities to make more of an effort themselves. He also emphasized the unacceptability of practices such as enforced marriages and female circumcision, which conflicted with basic British values. Blunkett launched proposals for language and citizenship classes for immigrants who wanted to become British citizens. The proposals in themselves were fairly innocuous: indeed, similar citizenship classes had recently been introduced as part of the national curriculum in British schools. Moreover, Blunkett drew parallels with naturalization procedures in the United States, Canada and Australia, widely perceived as classic multicultural societies; significantly, he avoided parallels with what might be seen as the more assimilationist practices of continental Europe. Nonetheless, the comments on integration and Blunkett's proposals for citizenship classes did amount to a clearer and more elaborate conception of the conditions for membership of British society and, as such, were highly significant. They challenged the traditional emphasis on racial discrimination as the central impediment to integration, suggesting instead that immigrants should 'do their bit' to ensure integration.

The proposals were greeted with scepticism by immigrant groups, as well as the Liberal Democrat Party. Interestingly, the latter's response was informed not so much by a basic commitment to individual freedom as by the practical consideration that it could have negative repercussions for race relations.[44] Most Conservative and Labour politicians welcomed the move, however, and the proposals became law under the 2002 Nationality, Immigration and Asylum Act. Arguably, this may represent the emergence of a new elite consensus which places more importance on problems of cultural differences among minority groups as a barrier to integration than on tensions caused by racial discrimination.

However, this shift in thinking also needs to be seen within the context of New Labour's views on social responsibility. This is a distinctively Blairite political philosophy which seeks to counterbalance the individualist rights-based ethos of the Thatcher era with an emphasis on what individuals should 'put back' into the community. Ethnic minorities are certainly not the only target of this approach – so too are parents, welfare recipients and those generally indulging in 'anti-social behaviour'. This emphasis on social responsibility has generated provisions for citizenship classes for British school children, as well as new nationals. The new emphasis on the responsibility of immigrants, then, may be as much to do with this broader agenda as with any new features of the immigrant integration problem *per se*.

## Other explanations for concerns about integration

The parallel between the debate in the UK on individual social responsibility and that on getting immigrants to 'do their bit' in the integration process is highly revealing. Both debates suggest an attempt to counter processes of social fragmentation and individualization by creating a stronger sense of collective identity and mutual responsibility. The discussion on individual responsibility urges individuals to take more account of how their actions affect their community; the debate on integration puts the onus on immigrants to make an effort to learn the language and culture of their receiving society. So both are in an important sense about contributing to a more cohesive community through developing a set of mutual obligations. This Blairite 'new communitarian' philosophy reflects anxiety about the process of social fragmentation which has been clearly discernible since the 1980s.

The debate on social fragmentation can help to make sense of the current discourse on immigrant integration. Looking at the integration problem from this perspective suggests just how difficult it is to isolate it from wider issues of social cohesion and identity. There are, as noted in the last section, very real social challenges linked to integration which require a serious rethink of existing approaches. But integration also seems to serve as an issue on which to pin responsibility for more general problems of social fragmentation and declining collective identities. Prominent among these are anxieties about the changing role of the state, especially its inability to act as guarantor of socio-economic security for all of its members, a development expressed most clearly in shrinking welfare provisions, persistently high unemployment and job insecurity since the 1970s. Other scholars have linked new forms of anxiety to the decline in collective identities and traditional bonds of solidarity such as class, church, ideology or nation-state. This gives rise to a search for new forms of collective identity, and may produce what Beck has termed a form of 'solidarity from anxiety'.[45] Whereas previous forms of solidarity or collective identity tended to be based on class alliances in order to promote more concrete material objectives, solidarity from anxiety is less coherent or rationally based. Lacking clear material goals, it tends to project diffuse and often ill-defined forms of insecurity onto symbolic targets, such as immigrants or ethnic minorities.[46] Hence the tendency to pin very vague concerns about employment, accommodation, schooling, social security, criminality and identity onto the immigration 'problem'.[47]

There are clear dangers in using integration issues to channel more diffuse anxieties: characterizing immigrants and ethnic minorities as problematic will hardly encourage them to develop a sense of identification or loyalty to host societies. Effective integration depends on an intensely subjective process of developing a sense of belonging and affinity, a process which is easily undermined by experiences of racism and exclusion. Stephen Castles has made this point in explaining the emergence of culturally defined ethnic communities, which he describes as a defensive reaction against the experience of discrimination and racism in receiving societies.[48] Castles argues that if immigrants had not encountered this form of exclusion, their integration into host societies would have progressed far more smoothly. Thus even well-meant attempts to promote integration through emphasizing the responsibilities of immigrants themselves may have a counterproductive effect. Putting immigrants and ethnic minorities on the defensive makes for a more hostile and highly charged debate, which may do more harm than good to processes of integration.

## INTEGRATION AND NEW LABOUR MIGRATION

We saw in Chapter 3 how popular concerns about migration control were drawn upon in Italy and to some extent in Germany in order to oppose further labour migration. However, in many senses the problem of integration can be even more readily marshalled as an argument against an increase in labour migration. After all, advocates of increased labour migration can easily draw a distinction between desirable economically productive workers and unwanted asylum-seekers and illegal immigrants, who are perceived to impose costs on the receiving society. But no such easy distinction is available concerning the integration problem, which, arguably, will be equally challenging for labour migrants, asylum-seekers, illegal immigrants or those coming to join their families. Here, advocates of increased labour migration will have to contend with two sets of concerns. The first is anxieties about a dilution of cultural identity through the immigration of large numbers of non-Europeans. These fears have been voiced in the German *Leitkultur* debate and in the Italian debate on the *extracommunitari*. And they have been expressed in the form of concerns about Muslim immigrants in all three countries. The second set of worries involves the socio-economic repercussions of failed integration, including problems of ghettoization, criminality, schooling and unemployment, and fears about the consolidation of an ethnic underclass.

### Integration challenges as an argument against increasing immigration: the case of Germany

Worries about increasing immigration have surfaced most clearly in Germany, where concerns about integration provide what is probably the CDU–CSU's most important argument against increased immigration. Politicians from these parties have consistently criticized the short-sightedness of accepting additional immigration without first ensuring that immigrants already in Germany are better assimilated. Their argumentation on this issue has drawn on both cultural and socio-economic concerns. One line of reasoning has been that (at least certain groups of) immigrants are failing to respect and absorb German language, norms and culture. A second line has been that immigrants are the source of socio-economic problems such as falling standards in schools, welfare costs and criminality. In both cases, the emphasis has been clearly on the failings of immigrant groups, which are considered unable or unwilling to integrate.

This was reflected in the CDU–CSU's response to the Süssmuth report, which the two parties criticized for failing to emphasize the importance of *Integrationsfähigkeit* (capacity to integrate) as a potential criterion for admission or long-term residence. They also opposed the report's proposals for expanding the possibilities for dual nationality and for introducing protection against the expulsion of immigrants' children who are responsible for crimes.[49] The tough approach on issues of *Integrationsfähigkeit* resurfaced in the debate on the *Zuwanderungsgesetz* (Migration Law), and especially the proposed classes for long-term immigrants on German language, culture and society. The CDU and CSU were keen that courses be compulsory, and wanted more robust penalties for failure to attend. They also proposed that the costs be shouldered by immigrants and employees rather than by the federal government or the *Länder*. The other issue of contention was the maximum age at which children brought up abroad would be entitled to join their immigrant parents in Germany. The CDU-CSU parties wanted a lower age limit, to avoid older children coming to join their parents with little knowledge of German language or culture (see Chapter 3).

CDU–CSU rhetoric on issues of integration was frequently, and self-professedly, populist. These parties pointed out that most Germans were anxious about the lack of integration of minority groups, and accused the SPD and the Greens of being out of touch with these concerns and unrepresentative of public opinion. In this sense, their tough assimilationist line on integration could be interpreted as an attempt to avoid the sort of elite-driven approach which appeared to have come unstuck in the Netherlands with the success of the Fortuyn List.[50] Indeed, as polls in spring 2002 indicated, most Germans were concerned about the impact of immigration on German society and thought that immigrants were unwilling to integrate.[51]

The CDU–CSU's arguments have also clearly pandered to simplistic assumptions about the causes of failed integration. CDU–CSU politicians have drawn on two principal sets of explanations for the apparent lack of *Integrationsfähigkeit*. According to some (albeit a minority), the source of the problem is one of apparently immutable cultural differences. Thus Kurt Biedenkopf, Minister President of Saxony, argued that acceptance of people from countries outside Europe would lead to a substantial change in German society and that the German population was not willing to accept this.[52] More frequently, though, the problem was located in other characteristics of immigrants – their 'socio-demographic profile', including language proficiency, skills, 'work mentality' and *Integrationskompetenz*.[53]

Whether the CDU–CSU and German elites in general opt for a cultural or a socio-economic conception of the causes of failed integration will have important repercussions for future labour migration policies. Assuming that economic and demographic pressures to recruit additional labour migrants become stronger in the coming years, the two conceptions would imply different criteria for selecting migrants. A socio-economic conception would be likely to favour high-skilled, middle-class immigrants with better chances of performing well in the labour market of receiving countries. A cultural conception would clearly favour immigration from Europe or other regions considered more culturally attuned to west European values. In reality, though, Germany may not be in a position to select immigrants on this kind of cultural basis. Quite apart from the political sensitivity in multi-ethnic societies of arguments based on cultural difference, there may simply be an insufficient supply of workers from eastern or southern Europe. The SPD–Green government discovered this, much to its chagrin, when there was limited up-take of the new Green Cards in eastern Europe. However, as wages and living standards in new EU member states and candidate countries rise, the attractiveness of moving to western Europe will decrease. So labour migration will almost certainly require accepting and integrating immigrants from more diverse cultural backgrounds.

Summing up the policy debate in Germany, the arguments about integration used by the CDU–CSU do seem to have had popular resonance. Although the issue played a less significant role in the 2002 elections than many expected, the constant threat that the Christian Democratic parties would 'play the immigration card' certainly kept the SPD on the defensive, making it retreat from a bolder defence of labour migration. But it remains to be seen whether the CDU–CSU will continue to pursue this line of argument, especially the emphasis on cultural questions. Indeed, one can discern a move away from culturally based arguments on problems of integration. The *Leitkultur* debate exploded in the CDU's face, and subsequent attempts to define *Integrationsfähigkeit* in terms of culture of origin are now the exception rather than the rule. Moreover, the shift towards a *ius soli* concept of citizenship in the 1990s appears to be irreversible. It is to be hoped that increasing possibilities for naturalization will embolden minority groups to make more assertive claims for their communities and in turn influence political elites to be more sensitive about employing exclusionary, ethnocentric or culture-based arguments.

Clearly, though, this will take some time. For now, one can expect the integration issue to remain one of the most important weapons in the arsenal of those opposed to increased immigration. The issue is vague enough to capture a range of anxieties about identity and values, welfare, education and criminality. What is open to question is whether growing demographic and economic pressures to accept more immigrants in the coming decades, as well as the impact of naturalization, will lead to a refocusing of the argument away from problems of cultural difference to problems of socio-economic inequality. In this case, for mainstream parties concerned about filling gaps in the labour supply, *Integrationsfähigkeit* will become more a question of having the right economic profile than of having a suitable cultural background.

### Integration versus additional labour migration?

To return to the central question posed at the outset, are concerns about the cultural and socio-economic impact of immigration likely to impede the introduction of more liberal policies? This will depend on how great the pressure is to recruit more labour migrants, and on whether there is elite (including cross-party) consensus on this need. British elites show signs that they will converge on this need, and German parties, despite some CDU–CSU qualms, may also be prepared to let economic contingencies prevail over concerns about integration, which are unlikely in the end to block the liberalizing agenda.

This is not to say that the integration issue will disappear from the political agenda. On the contrary, one can expect continuing debate on integration and a further rethink of integration strategies. Part of this may well represent a genuine attempt to address the real challenges of integration raised by previous and future immigration. In this respect, both Britain and Germany will need to give serious thought to preventing the recurrence of patterns of segregation and socio-economic exclusion among new immigrant communities. Neither country's model of integration is particularly well equipped for this task. The UK race relations model tends to be too focused on cultural impediments to equality as opposed to structural socio-economic constraints. The recent German emphasis on education and skills is constructive, but far more importance needs to be given to 'normalizing' cultural and ethnic diversity, and to tackling discrimination.

Neither of these deficiencies have much hope of being addressed if the public debate remains so highly politicized and emotive. In such a climate, there will always be a temptation to use proposals and reforms on integration as a way of diverting public anxieties about other issues, including the increased intake of labour migrants. In this case, we may see elements of the third scenario mentioned in the introduction: one in which the case for additional labour migration is accepted but is accompanied by a new discourse that is exclusionist on issues of cultural diversity.

Finally, in Italy there are no signs of an emerging elite consensus on integration, and the resulting lack of policy suggests that Italy will face serious problems in the future. The right wing continues to have incentives to mobilize support through crude ethno-cultural arguments, effectively precluding a serious debate on ethnic diversity and integration. As indicated above, there are other important traditions in Italian thought that emphasize social responsibilities to outsiders, and there is a clear business and trade union interest in incorporating labour migrants. But the ethical arguments based on social responsibility have provided fairly weak resistance to the right-wing agenda. Meanwhile, business interests may be content to continue to accept the current – albeit chaotic – pattern of illegal entry and subsequent regularization and the absence of a coherent strategy for integration. Perhaps it will require an alliance between these ethical and pragmatic elements to provide an effective counterweight to right-wing restrictionism and to create the conditions for a long-overdue debate on integration. Such pragmatic alliances have emerged among business and *Neue Mitte* or Third Way circles in Germany and the UK. In the meantime, however, arguments based on fears about cultural difference may well play a role in justifying a more restrictive agenda, although the salient and most pressing issue will remain that of controlling illegal immigration.

# 5

# *The international context*

National governments are under inordinate pressure to satisfy public demands in the area of migration policy. The politicization of migration issues in most west European countries has created incentives for political parties and the popular media to mobilize opinion around often unrealistic demands: watertight border control, the elimination of asylum abuse or zero immigration. Yet European states have found that their hands are tied. Introducing more restrictive migration controls can conflict with economic interests, while tighter borders and asylum systems can penalize genuine refugees. Faced with these pressures and constraints, governments have looked for forms of international cooperation that can help to address domestic migration management problems.

Two main forms of international cooperation are particularly important here: European Union attempts to develop common policies or approaches in the field of justice and home affairs (JHA), and cooperation with migrant-sending or transit countries to control, contain or prevent migration and refugee flows. West European states have also made use of their influence in international organizations to further migration policy goals – whether through the protection and assistance activities of the United Nations High Commissioner for Refugees (UNHCR), the work of the International Organization for Migration (IOM) on return and trafficking, or the EU's own external relations policy.

This chapter examines these various attempts at realizing domestic migration policy goals through international cooperation. Rather than running through a list of activities undertaken by various international fora or through bilateral relations, the chapter is organized according to the sorts of domestic goals that states seek to advance through international cooperation. Three types of policy goals are of particular importance. The first is forms of cooperation aimed at better migration management, including control of illegal entry and movement and attempts to combat the trafficking and

smuggling of people. The second type of cooperation aims to ensure a more even distribution of responsibilities between states, through forms of what I shall term direct or indirect burden-sharing. The third involves attempts to prevent unwanted flows occurring in the first place, through addressing the causes of migration or forced displacement.

Clearly, international and especially EU cooperation on immigration and asylum issues is not restricted to the areas of migration control, burden-sharing and prevention. Cooperation has emerged on a range of other issues, for example the treatment of third-country nationals in EU states, EU initiatives to combat racism and xenophobia or to develop anti-discrimination laws and, more recently, attempts to coordinate EU member states' policies in the area of recruiting labour migration. However, the central question addressed in this chapter is how far different forms of international cooperation can help to promote national policy goals by overcoming constraints faced by domestic policy-makers, or through helping to win public support from electorates. Migration management, burden-sharing and prevention represent the forms of cooperation with the greatest potential for meeting these goals. How far, then, can these forms of EU and international cooperation help to relieve governments of some of the domestic pressures they face and to alleviate public concerns about the new labour migration agenda?

## INTERNATIONAL COOPERATION AND MIGRATION MANAGEMENT

### Controlling illegal entry

Cooperation on border control and illegal entry was the first significant form of collaboration on internal security to emerge among European Community countries. It was born of necessity, as what one could term a 'spillover' from another area of EC cooperation: the Single European Act (SEA) of 1986, which set the goal of achieving the freedom of movement of goods, capital and workers between EC states by 1992. The free movement of persons within the EC clearly implied a weakening of border controls between member states. Five EC member states, France, West Germany and the Benelux countries, had already gone a step further in 1985, signing the Schengen Agreement to eliminate all internal border checks. This created pressure to adopt compensating measures to prevent illegal movement between EC states. As the Schengen Agreement expanded to include the southern European states, it also created an imperative to shore up more permeable sea borders.

Weaker internal borders made the EC, and especially the Schengen states, far more dependent on one another for effective immigration control. Greater interdependence also created a classic cooperation problem. Transit states within the EC had little incentive to apprehend illegal immigrants passing through their territory en route to other EC states. This was a source of concern for typical destination countries such as Germany, which received large numbers of asylum-seekers in the 1990s via other EC countries. West Germany and other states with relatively generous legislation on asylum appeared to be victims of the phenomenon of 'country shopping': the notion that asylum-seekers might be trying to move to the EU state with the most favourable reception conditions or the best chances to stay. One of the first important instruments adopted by EC countries, the 1990 Dublin Convention, aimed to address this problem of 'country shopping'. It established criteria for determining which state should be responsible for processing an asylum application, placing responsibility on states through which applicants had entered the EC.[1] However, when the Convention finally came into force in 1997, it proved almost impossible to implement in practice: it was difficult to prove the travel routes of applicants and the procedures for returning people to other states were cumbersome.

The second implication of weaker internal borders was that states became far more vulnerable to illegal entry via the Community's or the Schengen area's external borders. When the Schengen system was first agreed in 1985 this did not seem to constitute a problem. West Germany was the only member with a vulnerable external border, and one that was relatively well sealed. The removal of restrictions on movement from the Eastern bloc in 1989–90 and the accession of Italy, Spain and Greece to the Schengen Agreement made external borders far more vulnerable, however. There have been various attempts to strengthen external borders, mainly through cooperation between Schengen countries to define best practice on border checks and surveillance. States with external borders have been encouraged to develop more effective legislation, to improve infrastructure and equipment for carrying out border checks and to improve training for staff. There have also been attempts to encourage better information exchange between authorities within countries, as well as coordination between EU countries and with third countries.[2] Future EU member states in central and eastern Europe have meanwhile been under pressure to adopt these standards, and have received substantial financial assistance for upgrading border management systems, although often to the detriment of relations with countries outside the expanded Schengen area.[3]

In addition to border control, EU and especially Schengen countries have sought to control illegal entry through a range of other flanking measures: so-called 'pre-frontier control', which involves sending immigration and airline liaison officers to countries of origin and transit; harmonization of visa policies, including a common list of third countries whose nationals require a visa to enter the Schengen Area; harmonization of legislation on penalties for those transporting illegal immigrants; and readmission agreements with third countries, which are designed to facilitate the return of illegal immigrants from the EU to the third countries from which they have travelled. Cooperation in these fields has picked up since the late 1990s. The 1997 Treaty of Amsterdam created a more robust legal framework for instruments on immigration and asylum, and gave the European Commission a greater role in initiating proposals and overseeing implementation of the goals, which it has used to put forward a raft of new proposals. The Treaty of Amsterdam also set ambitious goals on border controls and visas and on combating illegal immigration (see Articles 62 and 63). Subsequent European Councils have defined cooperation in this area as a 'top priority' – the Seville Presidency Conclusions of June 2002 were particularly explicit on the need for rapid progress on border control, common visa policy and readmission.[4]

These measures have almost certainly made some contribution to controlling illegal movement into the EU. Member states have had to meet higher standards on border controls in land and sea ports, and Schengen members in particular have been under pressure to ensure better control. However, given the simultaneous rise in the numbers of those seeking to enter the EU illegally, these attempts at strengthening external borders do not appear to have led to an overall reduction in the number of illegal entrants.[5] Moreover, tighter control of Germany's and Austria's external borders appears to have shifted smuggling routes to south European sea routes. This form of smuggling by sea has been far more prone to sensationalist media coverage. Thus despite more intensive attempts to control external borders, the problem of illegal entry is in many ways far more of a popular concern in many EU countries than it was in the first half of the 1990s, before EU and Schengen cooperation had really gained momentum.[6]

It also remains doubtful whether the Dublin Convention has had much impact on the control of illegal flows *between* member states. The number of those returned to other EU states under the Convention has been extremely low, and it has been widely recognized that it has not achieved its goals. The EU has attempted to rectify this through establishing Eurodac, a system for comparing the fingerprints of asylum applicants and illegal immigrants. It has also been debating a new regulation, the so-called 'Dublin II', which revises the criteria for responsibility for assessing asylum claims and should facilitate procedures for readmission. But it remains doubtful how much of an incentive this will provide for states to be more effective in apprehending illegal immigrants in transit. All in all, cooperation on internal and external border controls has probably failed to compensate for the loss of national sovereignty over border controls for most countries.

The UK is particularly sensitive to these shortcomings, and has taken every opportunity to preserve national border controls; hence its non-participation in the Schengen Agreement, and its opt-out from many aspects of EU immigration policy. Indeed, the popular British media have had a near-obsessive preoccupation with the problem of the illegal entry of immigrants and asylum-seekers via continental Europe. This has been focused especially on the issue of Sangatte, an accommodation centre for illegal immigrants near the French port of Calais, whose residents frequently attempted to cross to Dover via the Eurotunnel. Interestingly, it was bilateral negotiations between the UK and France rather than EU arrangements which eventually produced a solution in December 2002, in the form of the closure of the centre and the distribution of its remaining occupants between the UK and France. But the British media and public remain highly sceptical about the benefits of EU cooperation on migration control, instead tending to see any loss of national sovereignty as a hindrance to effective migration control. Political elites have recently appeared to pin more hopes on the process of harmonization of member states' policies on asylum, in the expectation that creating a 'level playing field' will reduce the incentives for immigrants to pick the UK as a destination country (see the discussion of burden-sharing below). But cooperation on border controls and illegal entry certainly does not appear to be a vote winner for UK governments.

Germany too has tended to see itself as a 'magnet' country, bearing the brunt of more lax controls in other EU states. In the early and mid-1990s, as the number of asylum-seekers and immigrants coming to Germany rose dramatically, the government was keen to see more progress on EU policies in this area. It hoped that harmonization of legislation on asylum policies and better control of illegal flows would relieve it of some of this burden and compensate for the elimination of internal borders. However, EU attempts to harmonize policies proceeded only very slowly, and most other states showed little interest in the sort of burden-sharing schemes Germany proposed. As a consequence, Germany developed its own response to rising numbers of illegal immigrants, in part through the domestic changes discussed in Chapter 1 but also through bilateral relations with source and transit countries in central and eastern Europe. The key component of this response was its pioneering of the practice of readmission agreements with transit countries outside the EU in the early 1990s, ensuring that its neighbours to the east would take back migrants who had illegally entered into Germany via their territory. This has been widely perceived as playing an important role in reducing the number of asylum applicants in Germany since the mid-1990s, and it is a model that the EU has been trying to replicate in its relations with third countries.

For Italy, the SEA and the Schengen Agreement have brought mixed blessings. On the one hand, the elimination of internal borders has made it easier for illegal entrants to transit through Italy to Austria, France or Germany, and in this sense Italy has benefited from the Schengen Agreement. But it has almost certainly acted as an additional 'pull' factor for migrants who want to enter the Schengen or the EU area via Italy. Even if many of these illegal entrants do in fact move on to other states, the scale of illegal entry and the apparent unmanageability of Italy's coastline has generated a sense of near national crisis over the problem. Moreover, Italy has become an increasingly attractive destination country in its own right, and many migrants with the initial intention of moving on to other states eventually stay on.

A second major implication for Italy is that successive governments have been under intense pressure from EU or Schengen partners to control external borders more effectively. The need to conform to EU and Schengen standards on immigration and asylum policies and to step up border controls has been one of the primary factors influencing Italian policy since the late 1980s. Italy has consistently made attempts to secure financial and technical support from the EU for extra costs incurred in managing its coastal border. In May 2002 the government, building on a European Commission suggestion made the year before, proposed the creation of a European Border Guard.[7] Italy has received some funding from European Commission programmes, but its governments have been disappointed that more support is not forthcoming.

Like Germany, Italy has been forced to pioneer its own forms of international cooperation to respond to the problem of illegal immigration. One of these strategies has been to strengthen cooperation with sending and transit countries to the south and east of Italy. The government signed bilateral agreements with Morocco, Tunisia and Albania in 1998 under which these countries agreed to tighten controls on illegal outflows in return for additional development aid directed to reducing migration pressures.

The record of the EU and the Schengen states on successful cooperation to control migration through border and entry policies is therefore far from glowing. Given the economic and political imperative of eliminating internal borders, EU cooperation has certainly played some role in compensating for lost sovereignty over border control. Both Germany and Italy have at different times seen it as providing at least a partial solution to domestic shortcomings in the area of migration control. But cooperation among the EU and the Schengen states has serious limitations, and neither can boast a record that is particularly reassuring to public opinion in the EU.

## Combating trafficking

Joint efforts at combating the trafficking and smuggling of people may have greater potential to win public support. For a start, this area represents an obvious field for interstate cooperation: trafficking and smuggling networks are frequently transnational, and effective international coordination is in many cases vital for investigating, apprehending and prosecuting perpetrators. Moreover, cooperation in this area is less politically sensitive than that of border controls and entry, in that it does not involve loss of sovereignty over admission. It is also a fairly safe bet for winning domestic support. Efforts to combat dangerous and often exploitative trafficking or smuggling networks are unlikely to be subject to the same objections as more restrictive border controls or attempts to limit access to asylum systems. To be sure, many human rights and refugee groups have made the point that the use of smuggling or trafficking routes is often the only means by which refugees can enter the EU. But most are also concerned to prevent the types of exploitation many refugees are exposed to at the hands of traffickers and the often dangerous travel routes offered by smugglers. International cooperation in this area therefore has the potential to help realize domestic migration control goals as well as to reassure public opinion.

Cooperation to combat trafficking has involved a combination of 'preventive' and 'repressive' measures, as the European Commission characterizes them.[8] 'Preventive' measures could be defined as anything from addressing the root causes of migration and refugee flows (see below), to 'awareness-raising campaigns', alerting potential migrants of the risks of trafficking and smuggling, or the capacity-building of asylum systems in transit countries. Cooperation on 'repressive' measures includes interstate police and judicial cooperation to apprehend and prosecute perpetrators and the harmonization of legislation on penalties.

While there have been a number of measures under the rubric of prevention, it is not surprising that most progress has been made on 'repressive' measures. Since the Amsterdam Treaty came into force in 1999, the Council of Ministers has adopted a series of instruments setting out definitions of and penalties for trafficking and smuggling. At the same time, member states have launched a number of high-profile initiatives to combat trafficking and smuggling networks. The UK and Italy have both recognized the political mileage to be got from cooperation in this area, and have been at the forefront of efforts to intensify EU cooperation. In early 2001, for example, the British and Italian Prime Ministers, Tony Blair and Giuliano Amato, launched a well-publicized programme to combat smuggling and trafficking via the Balkans, deploying police and immigration officers in Bosnia to improve border checks. Italy has sent border guards to Albania to carry out pre-frontier checks. And in January 2003 both countries participated in Operation Ulysses, deploying ships to patrol the Mediterranean to apprehend illegal immigrants trying to cross into Spain and Italy.

The EU has also made cooperation on trafficking issues an important aspect of relations with third countries. It established cooperation frameworks to combat illegal immigration from China (in November 2000) and the western Balkans (in March 2001) and has initiated action plans for combating organized crime with Russia (2000) and with Ukraine (still to be finalized). Cooperation to combat trafficking and illegal migration is also part of the regional cooperation programme being discussed with the Mediterranean countries. The European Council stressed the importance of this form of cooperation with third countries at its 2002 meeting in Seville, insisting that 'any future cooperation, association or equivalent agreement which the European Union or European Community concludes with any country should include a clause on joint management of migration flows'.[9]

Some member states have even suggested that cooperation on such issues be a condition for receiving EU development assistance. At the Seville European Council Spain launched a controversial proposal to this effect, which was backed by the UK and other states. However, the proposal sparked widespread criticism from other governments, NGOs and even Tony Blair's own Minister for International Development. The UK was forced into an embarrassing retreat, and the Seville Conclusions contained a statement clearly rejecting such a form of conditionality for development aid.[10]

Thus while the UK government remains keen to underscore its commitment to cooperation on anti-trafficking measures, it also realizes that such measures can be controversial when they touch on other forms of collaboration with third countries which are traditionally the domain of the foreign and especially the development policy community. Paradoxically, this may imply focusing on 'repressive' rather than 'preventive' measures to combat the trafficking and smuggling of people. 'Repressive' measures involve forms of police and judicial cooperation which may well be less controversial than those requiring some reorientation of existing development programmes and thus likely to meet resistance from the development community.[11]

### BURDEN-SHARING

The second major area in which cooperation could address domestic concerns is that of burden-sharing: attempts to spread responsibility for and costs of receiving immigrants and asylum-seekers. The primary rationale for such forms of burden-sharing is to relieve states receiving larger numbers of refugees or illegal immigrants of some of the costs of reception. Burden-sharing may also reduce the risk and uncertainty associated with sudden changes in the level or direction of refugee or illegal migration flows. Thus a pre-agreed system of distribution could act as a kind of insurance system. Burden-sharing may be achieved through financial assistance or through a system of physical dispersal of asylum-seekers. I refer to such systems as 'direct' burden-sharing. Burden-sharing can also be promoted through measures to influence potential asylum-seekers or immigrants in their choice of country. For example, a convergence of asylum policies may discourage large numbers of asylum-seekers from applying to a country seen to be a 'soft touch', to use the popular British phrase. I refer to these sorts of approaches as 'indirect' burden-sharing.

Issues of burden-sharing have become more prominent in EU discussions since the introduction of the Schengen Agreement, the Single European Act, and cooperation in justice and home affairs. We have seen already how the elimination of internal borders made the question of responsibility for controlling irregular movement more topical. It became clear that the quality of migration control in one state would have major repercussions on flows into other states. But there were a number of other ways in which EU states began to be aware of the impact on each other of their actions in the area of migration control. Most explicitly, discrepancies between asylum rules in different EU countries appeared to be influencing the choice of destination for asylum-seekers, so that those countries with (or with what were perceived to be) relatively lax rules found themselves receiving larger numbers of asylum-seekers. Of course, legislation on asylum has certainly not been the only factor influencing the choice of country. But it has clearly played a large part in influencing patterns of flows, especially in cases where typically popular countries of asylum have suddenly introduced much stricter legislation. Most measures to promote burden-sharing have therefore focused on sharing responsibility for protection-seekers, that is asylum-seekers or refugees from civil war seeking temporary protection.

## Direct burden-sharing

Germany was the first country to raise these concerns seriously, in the early 1990s. It had experienced rising numbers of asylum-seekers from the late 1970s onwards, but those numbers began to escalate steeply in the first half of the 1990s. The major source of asylum-seekers in this period was refugees fleeing civil conflict in the former Yugoslavia: Germany received over 200,000 Yugoslavian applicants in 1992 alone. This figure was more than half of all applicants to EU countries. Simultaneously, it was receiving large numbers of *Aussiedler* from central and eastern Europe and hundreds of thousands of *Übersiedler*, who moved from eastern to western Germany. As we have seen, Germany responded to its immigration 'crisis' with a range of domestic reforms, in particular tightening rules on access to the asylum system and social conditions for asylum-seekers, streamlining assessment procedures and narrowing the criteria for recognizing claims. Although these measures did appear to have some impact on asylum flows – levels fell quite sharply in 1993 and 1994 – Germany nonetheless continued to receive far more asylum applications than any other EU state, with numbers remaining well above 100,000 per year until 1998. Against the backdrop of a difficult and expensive process of reunification, the public and politicians felt strongly that other EU states should help Germany by shouldering more responsibility for asylum-seekers and those fleeing civil conflict.

In 1994 Germany put before the Council of Ministers a proposal whereby people under temporary protection would be dispersed among EU states. The dispersal would be based on the three criteria of population, size of territory and GDP, in a system similar to Germany's own inter-*Länder* system of dispersal of asylum-seekers.[12] Predictably, the proposal won backing from a number of states such as Denmark and the Netherlands, which under such a system would receive fewer refugees than before. However, most states, including France and the UK, were wary about agreeing to a fixed formula for distribution and were, in any case, reluctant to sign up to a system that could imply receiving more refugees than at present. The proposal was also criticized by voluntary agencies, worried about the humanitarian implications of a compulsory form of physical dispersal of refugees. The proposal in its more rigid form was dropped. What emerged instead was a considerably diluted Council Resolution in September 1995 which outlined some of the considerations to be taken into account in determining how displaced persons could be 'shared on a balanced basis in a spirit of solidarity'.[13]

Despite this setback, the notion of burden-sharing was not abandoned. It appeared again in the Amsterdam Treaty. The language was again less than forthright: member states should 'promote a balance of efforts ... in receiving and bearing the consequences of receiving refugees and displaced persons'.[14] A similar formulation appeared in the directive on 'minimum standards for temporary protection in the event of a mass influx of displaced persons' adopted by the JHA Council in July 2001.

The issue of dispersal came to the fore again in the context of the Kosovo conflict. At the height of the refugee crisis in spring 2000, the UNHCR proposed a Humanitarian Evacuation Programme under which Kosovo Albanian refugees hosted by the Former Yugoslav Republic of Macedonia would be distributed among a number of receiving countries outside the region. In April, EU states met in Luxembourg to debate possible arrangements for the distribution of the refugees. Despite hopes that they would agree on a fixed formula for burden-sharing, ministers were able to agree only on a loose arrangement termed 'double voluntarism' under which each individual state could define its own quota of refugees. The outcome hardly represented a 'balance of efforts': the UK received just 4,346 refugees under the programme; France took 6,339 and Italy took 5,829. Predictably, Germany received far more than any other country, taking in 14,689 of the 52,853 evacuated to EU countries.[5]

There has been somewhat more progress in developing a system of financial redistribution between states, through the European Refugee Fund. This started in 1997 as a modest fund for providing grants to member states to support projects for asylum-seekers, refugees and displaced persons. In September 2000 its budget was increased to €216 million. The fund is intended to provide financial support proportionate to the number of asylum-seekers and refugees received by states, and to assist states with less developed facilities in improving their reception infrastructure and services. In this sense, it aims not only to compensate states for receiving greater numbers of refugees but also to help address one of the causes of a disproportionate distribution of refugees, that is discrepancies between standards of reception in different countries. It therefore involves both direct and indirect forms of burden-sharing.

In short, attempts to implement a system of direct burden-sharing have had only qualified success. States currently receiving lower numbers of refugees have limited incentives to sign up to a binding system of redistribution. Germany has thus been frustrated in its attempt to address domestic concerns through EU cooperation to ensure a balance of efforts. However, the issue has become less pressing for it in the past few years, as numbers of asylum applications have decreased. In contrast to the 1990s, Germany may now have more to lose than gain from more extensive burden-sharing. Interestingly, the UK has continued to resist a binding system of direct burden-sharing, despite the fact that it would now almost certainly benefit from such an arrangement. Instead, it has preferred to promote indirect burden-sharing through legislative harmonization, an approach which is discussed next.

## Indirect burden-sharing

It was already becoming apparent by the late 1980s that states with more generous asylum systems – higher standards of reception for asylum-seekers, lengthier application processes or less stringent criteria for recognizing refugees – were attracting larger numbers of asylum-seekers. Thus disparities in asylum systems were seen as penalizing countries with relatively generous rules. This not only placed an inordinate burden on states with more generous provisions, but also created a dangerous dynamic of competition between states keen to introduce more and more restrictive policies. Harmonization of asylum legislation was therefore seen both as a way of creating a 'level playing field' to ensure a more equal balance of responsibility between states, and as a means of halting a downwards spiral in standards of refugee protection and assistance.

The first real efforts at legislative harmonization took place in the early 1990s, once the 1992 Maastricht Treaty had established cooperation in JHA. The instruments adopted in this earlier phase of cooperation had a weak legal basis: they were resolutions, recommendations, decisions or common actions rather than more binding directives and regulations. Moreover, it quickly became evident that member states were not prepared to agree to common standards which would imply any significant liberalization of existing domestic provisions. What emerged, then, were a number of instruments which set common standards at the lowest common denominator of national provisions, and the process of harmonization gained a reputation among scholars and human rights groups as being highly restrictive. There were hopes that this would change with the 1997 Treaty of Amsterdam on European Union. The Treaty, which came into force in 1999, changed the legal basis for cooperation, introducing a more extensive role for the European Commission, the possibility of using more robust legal instruments and the potential to switch the decision-making procedure from unanimity to qualified majority voting. Member states also committed themselves to meet a number of deadlines for harmonizing policies, including those on minimum standards for the reception of asylum-seekers, asylum procedures, recognition of refugees and the granting of temporary protection.[16] Many expected this to speed up the process of harmonization and to encourage states to make the compromises necessary to avoid a 'lowest common denominator' approach.

But progress since Amsterdam has been disappointing. Certainly, the European Commission has been active in its expanded role, putting forward a plethora of proposals on the areas mentioned in the Treaty. It has developed methods for encouraging and monitoring harmonization, including a 'scoreboard' charting progress and a new 'open coordination method'[17] for approximating national legislation. A number of European Council meetings have also produced bold conclusions on the development of a common EU asylum and immigration policy. The 1999 Tampere special European Council on JHA was especially ambitious, calling for a common asylum procedure and for uniform status for those granted asylum. However, agreement on many of the proposed instruments has so far proved to be elusive. Harmonization of asylum policies, for instance, has continued to encounter resistance from many member states. By the beginning of 2003, only one European

Commission proposal on asylum, a directive on minimum standards for the reception of asylum-seekers, had been agreed on by the European Council. Provisions defining who qualified for refugee status and procedures for granting or withdrawing refugee status, tabled in 2001 and 2002 respectively, had yet to be agreed. Discussions in the Council suggested that there was still resistance to adopting instruments which would imply raising protection standards in some member states. Where approximation has occurred, it has continued to set common standards at a relatively low level, producing what has been referred to as a form of 'regressive harmonization'.[18]

Unlike in so many other areas of EU policy, the UK has been frustrated at the slow progress of harmonization of asylum policy. The British government sees the process as a means of achieving convergence of standards across the EU, so that Britain will no longer be a 'soft touch' on asylum compared to its continental neighbours. The argument has popular resonance, especially given widespread media reporting on how Britain has become the most attractive destination for asylum-seekers. But it is open to doubt whether harmonization would in fact generate the degree of burden-sharing the UK would like. As indicated above, research examining the reasons why asylum-seekers opt for particular countries of destination stresses the importance of a number of rather different factors: the existence of networks of friends and family, popular beliefs about the culture and society of the receiving country, previous colonial ties or a knowledge of English.[19] Legislation on asylum undoubtedly plays some role in influencing the choice of asylum country, but harmonization of EU-wide provisions, even if it were forthcoming, would not stop the UK from being an attractive destination.[20]

Germany has recently become less enthusiastic about harmonization than in the early 1990s, arguably because it no longer sees clear benefits to the process: asylum reforms in the 1990s have made Germany one of the more restrictive EU states, and harmonization may therefore necessitate the liberalization of some of its provisions. Any liberalization of asylum provisions would almost certainly be contested by the conservative opposition parties and would be difficult to sell to voters. Thus although the government has continued to declare its general support for a common asylum policy, it has been less forthcoming in supporting Commission proposals on asylum which would imply more generous rules on the definition of refugees or on the return of asylum-seekers to third countries.[21] Germany therefore opposed moves to qualified majority voting on asylum issues at the Nice European Council in December 2000.

Compared with the UK and Germany, Italy would probably be the most affected by harmonization in terms of having to introduce more generous domestic legislation. Italy's asylum laws are among the strictest in the EU, and in this sense harmonization would probably not be popular. However, unlike illegal migration and trafficking, the question of a common asylum policy is not prominent in public discussion on migration issues. It is difficult to predict how Italian political elites might respond to a more intensive process of harmonization of asylum legislation. On the one hand, they may want to follow an established pattern of aligning Italian provisions to common EU standards; on the other hand, given the highly politicized nature of the migration issue in Italy, populist political parties may want to block such moves.[22]

## PREVENTION

Like indirect forms of burden-sharing, preventive policies seek to alter the factors which influence people's migration decisions. Their goal is not to influence choice of country but rather to encourage or enable potential refugees or migrants to stay in their place of origin. In this sense, preventive policies can be seen as benefiting not only west European states but also the inhabitants of (potential) source countries. By addressing the causes of flight or migration, preventive policies would improve security and living conditions in countries of origin. With regard to economic migration, this would imply addressing typical socio-economic causes of movement, such as lack of job opportunities, low salaries, inadequate social and welfare services and poor infrastructure. With regard to potential refugees, it would imply mitigating the causes of flight, whether this be individual or group persecution or generalized conflict. Clearly, then, this type of prevention would involve applying a range of existing external policy tools, including development cooperation, protection of human and minority rights and conflict prevention.

There have been several proposals for this sort of preventive approach, or what have been termed measures to address the 'root causes' of migration, from the early 1980s onwards. The discussion was first initiated by Sadruddin Aga Khan in 1981 in his study on 'Human Rights and Massive Exoduses' for the UN Commission on Human Rights.[23] A number of scholars developed these themes further in the 1980s.[24] But the debate really took off in the early 1990s when a number of Western governments, the EU and certain UN agencies began to look for alternatives to traditional migration control policies.

One important factor influencing this shift of approach was an increasing awareness of the limitations of domestic and EU migration control policies. It was becoming clear for west European governments that restrictive entry policies, stricter border controls and tougher asylum systems alone would not solve the problem of unwanted flows. In fact, as already indicated, such restrictive measures conflicted with a range of economic goals and constitutional or human rights commitments. Thus many governments were looking for alternative means of limiting influx which would not conflict with domestic and international norms and goals. For human rights and refugee groups, the interest in preventive approaches was generated by a concern to avoid the problems for refugee protection created by restrictive asylum policies in Western states. Addressing the root causes of migration and refugee flows represented a far more humanitarian way of stopping unwanted flows than making asylum systems more restrictive or curbing access to west European states.

The shift towards preventive approaches was also linked to a new confidence in the possibilities for international action to address problems of human rights or civil conflict in sending countries. The end of the Cold War removed the high political and military risks associated with intervention, delinking such action from the threat of escalation into conflict between the two superpowers. Activities which were previously considered to constitute an unacceptable level of interference in the sovereign affairs of other states and thus a dangerous provocation became more feasible – as evidenced by UN, NATO or bilateral intervention in Iraq, Somalia, Bosnia and Herzegovina, Rwanda and, more recently, Kosovo; and by expanded international activities on human rights monitoring, capacity-building and post-conflict reconstruction.

The notion of prevention was not, however, without its shortcomings. First, as many commentators pointed out, there were clear practical limits to what external actors could do to address the causes of migration or flight. In the case of economic migration, the goal of a preventive approach would be no less than to reduce disparities between sending and receiving countries in terms of employment opportunities, salaries and socio-economic conditions, to a point where migrants would no longer have an incentive to emigrate to richer countries. Development policies had been striving for precisely these goals for decades; as these had such patchy success in so many countries, what reason was there to believe that migration prevention strategies would fare any better?

Secondly, a number of economists began to point out that economic development could generate an increase in emigration in the short to medium term, the so-called 'migration hump'. Economic restructuring often created unemployment and led to reduced welfare provisions, and could cause significant social upheaval. Meanwhile, increasing foreign investment and trade exposed more people to living conditions in wealthier Western states, creating incentives to emigrate.[25]

The first shortcoming implied that development assistance targeted towards preventing the causes of economic migration would be successful only if channelled to the 'good performers': countries with the capacity and will to introduce relevant economic, social and political reforms.[26] Moreover, if the goal were to prevent migration it would imply giving priority to major migrant-sending countries. This meant in effect those countries with significant minority groups already resident in western Europe, those with proximity to it, or those with traditional cultural, political or economic ties there. This form of prioritization was not popular with the development community, which obviously had its own criteria for allocating development aid.

The second consideration – the phenomenon of the 'migration hump' – implied that preventive policies would only kick in over the medium to long term. Migration prevention should in no way be perceived as a 'quick fix' for stopping flows. Thus preventive measures may have limited appeal to governments keen to reassure electorates that they are doing something to tackle unwanted migration. The timeframe required for such measures to have an impact on flows is simply too great to be of much electoral use.

The notion of preventing forced displacement presented equally serious challenges. Most efforts to address the causes of displacement tend to be undertaken once serious state repression is already occurring or violent conflict has already erupted. At this stage, it is far more difficult for external actors to exercise leverage on a repressive state which is struggling to retain its grip on power, or on parties to a civil conflict.[27] Often, the only feasible option for halting flight at this stage is military intervention, which can itself cause high numbers of casualties, trigger additional displacement and necessitate lengthy and expensive reconstruction programmes.[28] It therefore makes more sense to address the underlying causes of displacement, before repression or violence has escalated. But here one encounters different sorts of obstacles: notably, a lack of certainty in predicting where and under what circumstances conflict is likely to erupt, and a lack of political will to invest resources in problems which are not of immediate urgency.

Despite these constraints, a number of west European countries and the EU have shown interest in developing preventive strategies. Germany has more or less explicitly linked assistance activities in central and east European countries to the goal of preventing migration flows. Similarly, Chancellor Schröder was keen to point out that NATO intervention in Kosovo would have a benign effect on refugee flows to Germany. German governments have therefore used arguments about prevention as a means of justifying costly assistance programmes or unpopular military action to a sceptical public. Italy too has gained political mileage from its migration prevention policies. As mentioned earlier, it signed bilateral agreements with Morocco, Tunisia and Albania which included development assistance intended to stem emigration flows. It also led Operation Alba, a military intervention in Albania at the height of the political crisis in 1997, with the explicit aim of reducing refugee flows to Italy.

The UK, by contrast, has been more reticent about explicitly pursuing migration prevention policies. Unlike in Germany, the Foreign Office was reluctant to introduce refugee prevention as a rationale for intervention in Kosovo, preferring to keep the linkages more general: the concern was one of preventing a humanitarian crisis and a 'spillover' of the conflict to neighbouring areas. The Department for International Development too has been wary of the migration prevention agenda, for some of the reasons mentioned above. In particular, it has been concerned that such a strategy could divert resources from the most needy countries or could distort established development goals.[29]

Nonetheless, these types of preventive approaches have gained momentum at the EU level. The European Commission officials dealing with immigration and asylum matters began to advocate a 'root cause' approach as early as 1991, but their ideas were only developed seriously from 1998. In that year the Council set up a High Level Working Group (HLWG) on immigration and asylum. It was tasked with drafting action plans that would develop 'a comprehensive and coherent approach targeted at the situation in a number of important countries of origin or transit of asylum-seekers and migrants'.[30] The countries initially chosen were Afghanistan, Albania, Morocco, Somalia, Sri Lanka and Iraq, and most of the action plans were presented in 1999. Initially, there were worries about institutional and financial arrangements for implementing the plans, but in 2001 the European Parliament agreed to establish a budget of €10 million for implementing policies related to the 'external dimension' of JHA. It has since been extended to €15 million.

The work of the HLWG has not been without controversy. Specifically, it has been criticized by NGOs and the UNHCR for its focus on anti-trafficking and control measures rather than on cooperation with sending countries to address root causes. And a number of its activities also initially generated tension with the European Commission external relations community, which was concerned about the HLWG's lack of coordination with existing EU policies and its often undiplomatic approach to handling relations with third countries.

Despite continued reservations, the European Commission Directorates General for External Relations and Development have become increasingly involved in developing preventive approaches, especially since the Tampere Conclusions of 1999. The Conclusions called for the EU to integrate JHA matters into all areas of external relations. As the Conclusions stated,

The European Union needs a comprehensive approach to migration addressing political, human rights and development issues in countries and regions of origin and transit. This requires combating poverty, improving living conditions and job opportunities, preventing conflicts and consolidating democratic states and ensuring respect for human rights, in particular rights of minorities, women and children. To that end, the Union as well as Member States are invited to contribute, within their respective competence under the Treaties, to a greater coherence of internal and external policies of the Union.

This was reiterated later in the document, which stressed that

all competences and instruments at the disposal of the Union, and in particular, in external relations must be used in an integrated and consistent way to build the area of freedom, security and justice. Justice and Home Affairs concerns must be integrated in the definition and implementation of other Union policies and activities.[31]

Since then, Commission JHA, external relations and development officials have been working together to develop a new strategy for cooperation with sending countries which can address some of the EU's migration management concerns, but in a way that does not undermine existing development priorities or external relations. The approach seeks to take into account the concerns of third countries in the area of migration: the impact of reduced emigration on remittance flows from migrants, how selective migration policies attracting skilled workers to the EU can produce a 'brain drain', and sending countries' worries about the treatment of their nationals in EU member states.[32] As the Commission has pointed out, this more sensitive approach is required if the EU is to enlist cooperation from sending and transit countries.

This new Commission approach to migration flows has been most clearly developed in EU relations with the Mediterranean region. Cooperation on immigration issues has been an important aspect of the 'Barcelona Process', launched in 1995 as a framework for cooperation between the EU and 27 Mediterranean countries. Cooperation on migration embraces not only measures to combat illegal migration and trafficking (the typical control concerns of EU countries) but also questions of the integration of Mediterranean migrants in EU states, the impact of emigration on Mediterranean countries and the possibilities for addressing the causes of migration. This more 'global and balanced' approach was set out in a framework document on EU–Mediterranean cooperation on JHA, adopted in April 2002 at the Valencia European Council.[33] Meanwhile, the Commission's Country Strategy Paper for Morocco for 2002–4 contained the first explicit attempt to direct development aid towards preventing migration flows. The paper included a series of measures targeted at Morocco's northern provinces, which are the source of around 40 per cent of all Moroccan emigration to the EU. The programme set aside €70 million for projects designed to 'fixer les populations en créant de l'emploi dans les régions source principale de cette émigration'.[34]

However, there remain considerable divergences between EU member states over what shape 'integrated' external relations and migration policies should take. A number of states have been keen to focus on more short-term forms of prevention oriented towards migration control. Thus recent European Councils have put the onus more on cooperation to prevent illegal migration flows than on strategies for preventing the causes of migration. The Laeken and Seville European Councils both put special emphasis on control issues such as readmission and combating illegal migration, apparently retreating from the more 'root cause'-oriented tone of the Tampere European Council. Critics of the focus on combating illegal flows accuse the EU of attempting to contain flows in regions of origin rather than tackling their causes in a way which would be of mutual benefit to the EU and third countries.

Interestingly, the governments most keen to promote this type of containment strategy appear to be either those with a relatively weak tradition of development policy (such as Italy and Spain) or those whose development and foreign ministries are separate from their interior ministries (such as the UK). In both cases, development ministries or foreign ministries have enjoyed a less extensive role in shaping provisions on justice and home affairs priorities and are therefore less able to ensure that migration prevention policies are sensitive to the concerns and priorities of countries of origin. Migration prevention strategies which emerge from cooperative efforts between the development, foreign policy and migration management communities appear to be better equipped to factor in the concerns of sending countries and to develop longer-term, more sustainable approaches to prevention. Clearly, though, this type of more comprehensive and nuanced approach will not be a quick-fire success with electorates. Perhaps this partly explains why the European Commission has managed to pioneer such an approach, sheltered as it is from the political and electoral pressures faced by national ministers.

## 'Reception in the region' and resettlement

A second type of policy designed to influence migration flows to the EU is 'reception in the region', an approach which has featured prominently in discussions of possible 'alternative' approaches to migration management and refugee protection since the early 1990s. The idea here is to provide conditions in countries or regions of origin which prevent the need for refugees or internally displaced persons to seek protection further afield, that is in west European states. Thus the idea is not so much to remove the root causes of flight but, rather, to encourage people who do have to move to stay nearer to their home country.

As with preventive approaches, commentators are divided on the desirability of this sort of approach. Some have seen it as an innovative way of addressing the concerns of both refugees and Western receiving countries. It is regarded as more humane to allow refugees the option of obtaining adequate protection nearer to home rather than to force them to use smuggling or trafficking services to enter west European countries illegally. Critics of 'reception in the region' see it as an essentially selfish strategy of containment by Western governments. According to them, it represents a means of shifting responsibility for refugee protection to poorer countries and regions of origin, which are ill-equipped for hosting even larger numbers of refugees.

There have been various proposals for different models of burden-sharing over the past decade. The most modest proposals have suggested providing additional resources for the care and maintenance of refugees in camps in neighbouring countries. This would imply supporting the UNHCR or the host country in its regular protection and assistance activities, to ensure refugees do not have to seek asylum farther afield. More ambitious models for 'reception in the region' have advocated the establishment of 'safe havens' or 'safe areas' to provide protection for refugees or internally displaced persons in civil conflict. Other proposals have suggested establishing 'internationally protected areas' (IPAs), which would be leased from host countries by the UN or by groups of states.[35] These models may include the possibility of European states' returning refugees or asylum-seekers to 'safe areas' or IPAs without violating principles of international refugee law. They may also include possibilities for screening refugees in first countries of asylum through national consulates and granting 'protected entry visas', to allow them access to Western states.[36]

It has been suggested that these schemes could also be combined with expanded quotas for the resettlement of particularly vulnerable or high-risk cases from regions of origin. This notion of resettlement has recently generated interest on the part of some EU countries, including the UK. The rationale is clear enough. The expectation is that resettlement would offer a better way of addressing migration management problems while still offering protection to refugees. Many people who manage to reach west European countries and seek asylum are not in need of international protection, while some of the most vulnerable victims of conflict or persecution are simply unable to gain access to asylum systems. Thus a screening process in the region would enable at least a portion of those in need of protection to reach safety. At the same time, resettlement may be seen as a way of limiting the need for illegal migration. If people are able to seek protection through official channels near their place of origin, so the argument runs, then they will not need to make use of people-smugglers or -traffickers to make the journey to west European states.

The UK Home Office is still deliberating about different possibilities for an expanded resettlement scheme. Although such a scheme would almost certainly be of assistance to refugees in regions of origin who lack the strength or resources to move, it is unlikely to lead to a substantial reduction in the number of asylum-seekers arriving in western Europe. For a start, it would not reduce 'push' factors for economic migrants keen to enter west European countries. Moreover, as most studies have concluded, a regional processing scheme could not act as a substitute for asylum systems in receiving states. Resettlement or regional processing schemes are bound to be imperfect, and asylum countries will need to keep access open for asylum-seekers arriving on their territory. For these reasons, although resettlement may address the protection needs of some of those unable to move, it will not solve the problem of migration management.

### CONCLUSION

Interstate cooperation on migration issues has on the whole had limited success in meeting domestic goals of migration management, burden-sharing and prevention. To be sure, common efforts to combat illegal migration may have limited some influx, but this has largely been offset by the overall rise in levels of flows. Efforts at burden-sharing, although still in their infancy, are probably having an impact (albeit limited) on the sharing of costs. But states receiving fewer asylum-seekers or illegal immigrants remain sceptical about committing themselves to any scheme implying substantial redistribution, and preventive measures have yet to demonstrate any clear impact on migration or refugee pressures in countries of origin.

West European governments have on the whole been keen to draw public attention to their efforts at international cooperation and the ways in which these efforts might help to address the shortcomings of domestic policy. Germany has been an enthusiastic supporter of harmonization and burden-sharing in the past, but is less so now that its restrictive asylum legislation appears to have reduced numbers of asylum-seekers. The Italian and UK governments have both drawn attention to their interstate initiatives for combating illegal migration and people-smuggling.

But there are reasons to be sceptical about how far such forms of cooperation can really allay public concerns about migration and asylum in west European states. And herein lies a dilemma for west European governments. On the one hand, cooperation aimed primarily at stopping unwanted immigration and containing refugees in regions of origin may mollify public opinion in the short to medium term. But it will not address the causes of flows, and may in many cases even produce counterproductive results. Purely control-oriented approaches may simply encourage more dangerous smuggling practices and drive this lucrative business into the hands of more organized and sophisticated smuggling and trafficking networks. Nor will an exclusive focus on issues of migration control in relations with third countries be the best tactic for enlisting support from sending and transit countries. Attempts to contain refugees in regions of origin may also have negative repercussions for relations with first countries of asylum, and in some cases they may be destabilizing for the host country. Thus although a focus on control and containment may have more immediate popular resonance, it will not offer a sustainable solution to the problem.

On the other hand, the types of cooperation which may reduce flows in the longer run are likely to lack electoral appeal. Such measures would include more investment in development programmes aimed at reducing emigration pressures in the medium to long term; more creative approaches to channelling remittances and maximizing the positive impact of emigration on development; and immigration policies which are far more sensitive to the problem of 'brain drain' in source countries. Such approaches would provide a better basis for cooperation with sending countries and would aim to ensure that migration contributes to development, or at the very least does not undermine it. This type of thinking can be found in the Commission's recent attempts to integrate migration issues into the EU's external policy. It has probably been most clearly developed in the framework of the Euro-Med process, especially in the Union's relations with Morocco.

But the ability of the Commission to adopt this type of approach reflects at least partly its unique position as a bureaucracy unconstrained by considerations of electoral politics. Commission officials can afford to take a longer view. Most officials in national justice and interior ministries cannot. And as long as migration remains such a highly charged political issue, west European governments will have little immediate incentive to invest in these types of approaches. Instead, we may continue to see forms of cooperation that place the onus on combating trafficking and illegal flows and on readmission agreements, pre-frontier control and reception in the region. Such approaches will place an increasing burden on poorer sending countries to readmit illegal migrants, manage borders or host refugees. Meanwhile, the competition to attract highly skilled immigrants may well increase the problem of 'brain drain' from developing countries, which can ill afford to lose their most skilled nationals. Thus poorly thought out and short-term approaches to cooperation with sending countries may well undermine development and, if anything, contribute to the factors generating migration flows.

# Conclusion

In spite of their many differences, Germany, the UK and Italy are each facing a conflict between an economically driven demand for labour migration and political pressures for restriction. The tension is manifested in varying forms in the three countries, with each displaying a somewhat different constellation of pro- and anti- labour migration interests and pressures and a different pattern of discourse on the issue. However, the basic conflict in each case is one between liberal, centre-left and pro-business advocates of increased labour migration to fill gaps in the labour market and offset ageing populations on the one side, and, on the other, protectionist, conservative or right-wing populist protagonists arguing that such a policy would threaten native jobs, welfare systems, security or national identity.

It is tempting to characterize this conflict as a tension between a rational, utilitarian response to socio-economic needs, and a more visceral politics of fear. After all, much of the anti-immigration argumentation appears to be based on an exaggerated and often misinformed understanding of the costs and impact of immigration. Such argumentation frequently taps into diffuse fears about socio-economic or political change or declining social cohesion, phenomena which have little to do with immigration *per se*. But while there is some truth in this characterization, it would be wrong to dismiss these concerns. There are indeed tangible, albeit overstated, control problems generated by illegal flows and asylum systems, just as there are very real social problems linked to failed integration. Thus although political mobilization of these fears may grossly inflate the problem, these concerns do need to be taken seriously. Governments in western Europe will need to strike a balance between responding to the politics of anxiety and meeting demographic and economic needs.

The three cases examined in this book each show how influential this politics of anxiety has been in shaping migration policies. However, one can also discern important and growing counter-tendencies which militate against pressures for restriction. One of these is obviously economic and demographic pressures to liberalize labour migration policies. Other counter-forces are the domestic or international commitments embedded in democratic and human rights norms and institutions. But there is also an increasingly important role to be played by long-term resident ethnic minorities in most west European states. These communities may not always mobilize for specific demands or for more generous entry policy but they still exert indirect influence on the discussion of migration. Their very presence and expanding political rights render racist or ethnocentric positions less and less tenable. In this sense, multicultural societies may not necessarily become more generous in their entry policies, but they will nevertheless find some of their policy options constrained, notably those relating to criteria for admission and naturalization or for models of integration.

What does all this imply for the three scenarios outlined in the introduction to this book? Will pressures for restriction block the emergence of expanded labour migration policies; will they decline as national publics recognize the economic benefits of migration; or will such pressures be transferred instead onto other categories of excluded immigrants?

The case of Italy appears to be the most fluid and uncertain of the three. The current Casa delle Libertà government is attempting to juggle populist pressures for restriction with a business-friendly agenda. Indeed, Berlusconi's style of politics is the epitome of a populist catch-all politics, combining official hardline restrictive measures with de facto toleration of illegal immigrants. This dual approach may be possible only in a country such as Italy, where there is a well-established pattern of tolerating and regularizing illegal immigrants as a means of meeting demand for migrant labour. In this context, toleration of illegal entry and labour combined with periodic regularizations may well be a sustainable way of meeting labour demand. And given the current weak showing of centre-left opposition parties on migration issues, it may also be politically viable in the medium and even long term. However, it is certainly not optimal from the point of view of the living conditions and legal status of irregular migrants, nor is it an effective means of addressing the problem of migration control. Moreover, this approach is likely to come under increasing attack from other EU member states, keen to ensure that Italy does not create a 'pull' factor for would-be illegal immigrants. For now, however, Italy clearly fits into the first scenario of blocked labour migration reforms, although with a simultaneous toleration of high levels of illegal migrants.

The UK, by contrast, appears to conform to the third scenario: labour migration reforms are emerging but elite consensus is certainly not taking migration issues off the political agenda. Instead, more generous rules on labour migration are consistently packaged with more draconian measures to restrict illegal immigration, conditions for asylum-seekers and access to the asylum system. Thus far, the Labour government has found that its labour market reforms are relatively uncontroversial. It has benefited from almost full employment, an acquiescent opposition party and fairly limited domestic institutional constraints on policies to crack down on illegal migrants and asylum-seekers. But this will not necessarily continue to be the case, especially in the likely event of increasing demand for unskilled labour. Once the government has exhausted the repertoire of feasible restrictive measures for illegal migration and asylum-seekers, it is difficult to see where it can turn to in order to mollify anti-migration forces. There are indications that it will look more and more to international solutions such as reception in the region and resettlement, combined with more extensive use of return. These alternative options for reconciling migration management goals and protection concerns do have a certain neat logic. Each of them, however, has its shortcomings, and none can provide a panacea to the control versus protection dilemma.

Germany appears to be wavering between the first and third scenarios. The SPD–Green government did attempt to liberalize labour migration policies, but so far it has been blocked by the CDU–CSU opposition. The Christian Democrat parties have marshalled a range of arguments against increased legal migration, including the perceived competition for jobs of indigenous workers and problems of integration. But this opposition is unlikely to be sustained should these parties find themselves in power and under pressure from business to fill labour gaps in important sectors. In this case, Germany may begin to move closer to the British position, with elite consensus on the need for (at least skilled) labour migration, but continued pressure to restrict access for non-economically beneficial categories of migrants and refugees. Yet a number of factors suggest that such a consensus will be more difficult to achieve than in the UK: notably, the more protectionist inclinations of both Social and Christian Democratic parties; the lessons learned from the unintended consequences of labour migration in the guest-worker era; and a reluctance in many quarters to accept the fact of multiculturalism. Thus Germany may well continue to fluctuate between the first and third scenarios.

All this suggests that the second scenario of a depoliticization of migration issues is the least likely to emerge. The only condition under which such a scenario could arise would be a cross-party agreement – backed by the popular media – to remove migration issues from electoral politics. I have argued in this book that there are limited incentives for political parties to commit themselves to any such agreement. Even in the event of a huge demand for additional labour migration in the future, political parties will still have a strong interest in mobilizing electoral support by promising more restriction of other types of migration. And there is every indication that such mobilizing strategies will continue to be successful with sections of the electorate who are anxious about the socio-economic and cultural impact of migration. Migration issues appear to provide a perfect vehicle for channelling diffuse socio-economic, political and identity-related anxieties.

The best hope is that restrictive control measures are developed sensibly and take into account their multiple impacts on migrants, refugees and both sending and receiving societies. For there is much at stake in the development of migration control policies. They will have major repercussions for refugee protection and human rights, inter-ethnic relations and integration, economic growth and, not least, development and stability in sending countries. West European governments will need to be sensitive to these externalities of migration control policies. In particular, they would be well advised to give more serious thought to the future shape of international cooperation on migration control. Efforts at international cooperation to manage migration flows need to be based on a better understanding of the relationship between migration and development and must take into account the interests and concerns of migrant-sending countries. The alternative would be to maintain the current focus on short-term restriction measures. This may have electoral appeal, but it would do little to alleviate the burden on sending and transit countries or to address the causes of illegal migration or refugee flows.

# Notes

INTRODUCTION

1 A more detailed discussion of the demographic argument for increased labour migration is provided in Chapter 2.

2 In particular, the distinction between asylum-seekers, illegal migrants and refugees is often confused in public debate. One reason for this is that a large proportion of asylum-seekers enter European countries illegally or become illegal if they do not respect deportation orders once their applications have been rejected. In fact, regardless of how they have entered west European countries, once illegal immigrants have applied for asylum they receive the legal status of asylum-seekers. They are allowed to stay for the duration of their application procedure, although in many cases they are not allowed to work. If their applications for asylum are accepted, they become recognized refugees, with legal residence status and an entitlement to work. Others may have their asylum applications rejected but may nonetheless be allowed to stay under another status, such as temporary protection or humanitarian status. The term 'long-term residents' refers to immigrants who have not become citizens, although they have lived in the host country for a number of years, or may even have been born there. The term 'ethnic minority groups' also includes those who have been naturalized or who were born citizens of the host country.

3 See, for example, Julie R. Watts, *Immigration Policy and the Challenge of Globalization: Unions and Employers in Unlikely Alliance* (Ithaca, NY and London: ILR Press, 2002). As Watts explains, unions in many countries have become increasingly concerned about protecting legally employed workers from being undercut by irregular labour migrants. The latter usually accept lower salaries and worse working conditions or they involve lower social costs for employers, thus competing against those who are legally employed.

4 Ulrich Beck, *Risk Society: Towards a New Modernity* (London: Sage, 1992).

5 See Chapter 4 for a fuller discussion of these concepts.

6 Paul Statham, *The Political Construction of Immigration in Italy: Opportunities, Mobilisation and Outcomes* (Berlin: Wissenschaftszentrum Berlin für Soziale Forschung, 1998).

7 Tomas Hammar, *European Immigration Policy* (Cambridge: Cambridge University Press, 1985).

1 THE EVOLUTION OF POSTWAR EUROPEAN MIGRATION POLICIES

1 For the classic description of clientelist models of migration policy-making, see Gary P. Freeman, 'Modes of Immigration Politics in Liberal Democratic States', *International Migration Review*, Vol. 29, No. 4, 1995, pp. 881–902.

2 Ulrich Herbert, *Geschichte der Ausländerpolitik in Deutschland: Saisonarbeiter, Zwangsarbeiter, Gastarbeiter, Flüchtlinge* (Munich: Verlag C. H. Beck, 2001), p. 204.

3 Christian Joppke, *Immigration and the Nation-state: The United States, Germany and Great Britain* (Oxford and New York: Oxford University Press, 1999), p. 65.

4 Herbert, *Geschichte der Ausländerpolitik in Deutschland*, pp. 209–10.

5 Joppke, *Immigration and the Nation-state*, p. 62.

6 Saskia Sassen, *Guests and Aliens* (New York: The New Press, 1999), p. 102.

7 Gary P. Freeman, *Immigrant Labor and Racial Conflict in Industrial Societies: The French and British Experience 1945–1975* (Princeton, NJ: Princeton University Press, 1979).

8 Sarah Collinson, *Europe and International Migration* (London: Royal Institute of International Affairs/Pinter Publishers, 2nd edn, 1994), p. 45.

9 See, for example, James F. Hollifield, 'Immigration and Republicanism in France: The Hidden Consensus', in Wayne A. Cornelius, Philip L. Martin and James F. Hollifield (eds), *Controlling Migration: A Global Perspective* (Stanford, CA: Stanford University Press, 1992), pp. 152–6.

10 Marcelo M. Suárez-Orozco, 'Anxious Neighbors: Belgium and its Immigrant Minorities', in Cornelius et al. (eds), *Controlling Migration*, p. 243.

11 Heinz Fassmann and Rainer Münz (eds), *European Migration in the Late Twentieth Century* (Laxenburg: International Institute for Applied Systems Analysis, 1994), p. 7.

12 Freeman, *Immigrant Labor*, pp. 179–82.

13 This refers to former colonies that joined the Commonwealth after the Second World War following independence, as opposed to the Old Commonwealth former dominions of Australia, Canada and New Zealand.

14 Peter Hennessey, *Never Again: Britain 1945–1951* (London: Vintage, 1993), p. 442.

15 Ibid., pp. 442–3.

16 Collinson, *Europe and International Migration*, p. 47.

17 Freeman, *Immigrant Labor*, pp. 256–7.

18 See, for example, Zig Layton-Henry, *The Politics of Immigration: 'Race' and 'Race' Relations in Postwar Britain* (Oxford: Blackwell, 1992), pp. 39–79.

19 Joppke, *Immigration and the Nation-state*, pp. 70–72.

20 Article 1A, Convention Relating to the Status of Refugees, Geneva, 28 July 1951 (189 UNTS 137).

21 See, for example, James C. Hathaway, *The Law of Refugee Status* (Toronto and Vancouver: Butterworths, 1991), pp. 7–8.

22 Paul Weis, *The Refugee Convention, 1951: The Travaux Préparatoires Analysed* (Cambridge: Cambridge University Press, 1994), p. 335.

23 Sandra Lavenex, *The Europeanisation of Refugee Policies: Between Human Rights and Internal Security* (Aldershot, Hants: Ashgate, 2001), p. 38.

24 Collinson, *Europe and International Migration*, p. 40.

25 Adrian Favell, *Philosophies of Integration: Immigration and the Idea of Citizenship in France and Britain* (London: Macmillan Press, 2nd edn, 2001), pp. 110–11.

26 Cited in Layton-Henry, *The Politics of Immigration*, p. 184.

27 See, for example, Martin O. Heisler and Zig Layton-Henry, 'Migration and the Links between Social and Societal Security', in Ole Weaver, Barry Buzan, Morten Kelstrup and Pierre Lemaire (eds), *Identity, Migration and the New Security Agenda in Europe* (London: Pinter Publishers, 1993), pp. 157–8; and Stephen Castles, 'The Racisms of Globalization', in Stephen Castles (ed.), *Ethnicity and Globalization: From Migrant Worker to Transnational Citizen* (London: Sage, 2000), pp. 180–82.

28 Favell, *Philosophies of Integration*, 109–10.

29 Herbert, *Geschichte der Ausländerpolitik in Deutschland*, pp. 221–3.

30 Ibid., pp. 222–8.

31 Joppke, *Immigration and the Nation-state*, p. 78.

32 Thomas Faist, 'How to Define a Foreigner? The Symbolic Politics of Immigration in German Partisan Discourse, 1978–1992', in Martin Baldwin-Edwards and Martin A. Schain (eds), *The Politics of Immigration in Western Europe* (Ilford: Frank Cass, 1994), p. 57.

33 Herbert, *Geschichte der Ausländerpolitik in Deutschland*, p. 255.

34 Joppke, *Immigration and the Nation-state*, p. 84.

35 Simone Wolken, *Das Grundrecht auf Asyl als Gegenstand der Innen- und Rechtspolitik in der Bundesrepublik Deutschland* (Frankfurt am Main: Peter Lang, 1987), p. 39.

36 Lavenex, *The Europeanisation of Refugee Policies*, pp. 45 and 66.

37 Joppke, *Immigration and the Nation-state*, p. 188.

38 Lavenex, *The Europeanisation of Refugee Policies*, p. 60.

39 Ibid., p. 63.

40 James F. Hollifield, 'Ideas, Institutions, and Civil Society: On the Limits of Immigration Control in France', in Grete Brochmann and Tomas Hammar (eds), *Mechanisms of Immigration Control: A Comparative Analysis of European Regulation Policies* (Oxford and New York: Berg, 1999), p. 78.

41 John W. P. Veugelers, 'Recent Immigration Politics in Italy: A Short Story', in Martin Baldwin-Edwards and Martin A. Schain (eds), *The Politics of Immigration in Western Europe* (Ilford: Frank Cass, 1994), p. 34.

42 Giovanna Zincone, 'Immigration to Italy: Data and Policies', in F. Heckmann and W. Bosswick (eds), *Migration Policies: A Comparative Perspective* (Stuttgart: Enke, 1995), p. 137.

43 Veugelers, 'Recent Immigration Politics in Italy', p. 35.

44 Ibid., p. 37.

45 Anna Triandafyllidou, 'Nation and Immigration: A Study of the Italian Press Discourse', *Social Identities*, Vol. 5, No. 1, 1999, p. 73.

46 OECD SOPEMI, *Trends in International Migration* (Paris: OECD, 1999), p. 145.

47 Hollifield, 'Ideas, Institutions, and Civil Society', pp. 59–95.

48 See, for example, Jesuit Refugee Service Dispatches, *Refugee News Briefings*, No. 54, 30 July 1999 (see *www.jesref.org*).

49 Commission for Racial Equality, *Asylum-seekers and Race Relations: The Commis-*

*sion for Racial Equality's View*, 14 April 2000 (see *www.cre.gov.uk/misc/Asylnote. html*).

50 Herbert Dittgen, 'Immigration Control: Some Observations on National Traditions, Internal and External Controls and Policy Paradigms', in Axel Schulte and Dietrich Thränhardt (eds), *International Migration and Liberal Democracies* (Münster: Lit Verlag, 1999), p. 81.

51 Hollifield, 'Ideas, Institutions, and Civil Society', p. 82.

52 On the debate on the impact of enlargement on the free movement of people, see Christina Boswell, *EU Enlargement: What are the Prospects for East-West Migration?*, European Programme Working Paper (London: Royal Institute of International Affairs, November 2000).

53 The Schengen Agreement, adopted in 1985 by France, Germany and the Benelux countries, abolished internal border checks between its member states. The agreement came into force only in 1995. Since 1990, a number of other EU states and Norway and Iceland joined the Schengen area, and in 1997 it was incorporated into the EU framework through the Treaty of Amsterdam. For a fuller discussion, see Chapter 5.

54 See, for example, Saskia Sassen, *Losing Control? Sovereignty in an Age of Globalization* (New York: Columbia University Press, 1996), p. xiv; and James F. Hollifield, *Immigrants, Markets and States: The Political Economy of Postwar Europe* (Cambridge, MA: Harvard University Press, 1992).

55 See Chapter 5 for a more detailed discussion.

56 Secretariat of the Inter-governmental Consultations on Asylum, Refugee and Migration Policies in Europe, North America and Australia, *Working Paper on Reception in the Region of Origin* (Geneva: IGC, 1994); and Gregor Noll, Jessica Fagerlund and Fabrice Liebaut, *Study on the Feasibility of Processing Asylum Claims Outside the EU against the Background of the Common European Asylum System and the Goal of a Common Asylum Procedure*, Final Report (Brussels: European Community, 2002).

57 European Council, *Presidency Conclusions*, Tampere, 15–16 October, SN 200/99 (1999).

58 David Kyle and Rey Koslowski, 'Introduction', in David Kyle and Rey Koslowski (eds), *Global Human Smuggling: Comparative Perspectives* (Baltimore and London: Johns Hopkins University Press, 2001), p. 4.

59 Heather Grabbe, 'The Sharp Edges of Europe: Extending Schengen Eastwards', *International Affairs*, Vol. 76, No. 3, July 2000, pp. 519–36.

## 2 NEW POLICIES ON LABOUR MIGRATION

1 On the classic thesis of states' ambivalence on migration control, see Wayne A. Cornelius, Philip L. Martin and James F. Hollifield (eds), *Controlling Migration: A Global Perspective* (Stanford, CA: Stanford University Press, 1992).

2 See, for example, Saskia Sassen, *The Mobility of Labor and Capital: A Study in International Investment and Labor Flow* (Cambridge and New York: Cambridge University Press, 1988); Saskia Sassen, *Losing Control? Sovereignty in an Age of Globalization* (New York: Columbia University Press, 1996); Peter Stalker,

*Workers without Frontiers: The Impact of Globalization on International Migration*
(Boulder, CO and London: Lynne Rienner, 2000); and Bimal Ghosh, *Gains from Global Linkages: Trade in Services and Movements of Persons* (Basingstoke: Macmillan in association with IOM, 1997).

3 Sassen, *The Mobility of Labor.*
4 Stalker, *Workers without Frontiers*, p. 117.
5 Sassen, *Losing Control?*, pp. 76, 80–2.
6 Henk Overbeek, *Globalization and Governance: Contradictions of Neo-Liberal Migration Management*, HWWA Discussion Paper 174 (Hamburg: Hamburg Institute of International Economics, 2002).
7 Manuel Castells, 'Information Technology and Global Capitalism', in Will Hutton and Anthony Giddens (eds), *Global Capitalism* (New York: The New Press, 2000), p. 52.
8 Anthony Giddens and Will Hutton, 'In Conversation', in Will Hutton and Anthony Giddens (eds), *On the Edge: Living with Global Capitalism* (London: Vintage, 2001), p. 22.
9 Sandra Lavenex, 'Skilled Labor and European Immigration Policies: A Shift of Paradigms?', paper presented at the International Studies Association annual meeting, New Orleans, 23–27 March 2002, p. 19.
10 Castells, 'Information Technology and Global Capitalism', p. 54.
11 Sassen, *Mobility of Labour*, p. 22.
12 Ghosh, *Gains from Global Linkages*, p. 29.
13 For an analysis of the provisions of this agreement, see Sandra Lavenex, 'Labour Mobility in the General Agreement on Trade in Services (GATS) – Background Paper', PEMINT Working Paper 1/2002 (2002). (PEMINT is an EU-sponsored research project on the Political Economy of Migration in an Integrating Europe.)
14 David Held, 'Democracy and Globalization', in Daniele Archibugi, David Held and Martin Köhler (eds), *Re-imagining Political Community: Studies in Cosmo-politan Democracy* (Cambridge: Polity, 1998), p. 17.
15 Lin Leam Lin, 'International Labour Movements: A Perspective on Economic Exchanges and Flows', in Mary M. Kritz, Lin Leam Lin and Hania Zlotnik (eds), *International Migration Systems – A Global Approach* (Oxford and New York: Oxford University Press, 1992), p. 141.
16 European Commission White Paper on *Completing the Internal Market*, COM (85) 310 (Brussels: Commission of the European Communities, 1995).
17 See, for example, Stephen Glover et al., *Migration: An Economic and Social Analysis*, RDS Occasional Paper no. 67 (London: Home Office, 2001), p. 5.
18 See, for example, Rudolf Winter-Ebner and Josef Zweimüller, 'Do Immigrants Displace Young Native Workers? The Austrian Experience', *Journal of Population Economics*, Vol. 12, No. 2, 1999, p. 329.
19 An alternative possible repercussion of migration by unskilled labour is that it can exercise a (usually very slight) downward pressure on salaries in some sectors. However, a number of experts have argued that this phenomenon is largely theoretical, as there is little evidence of such an effect, even after a large-scale influx of migrants. See David Card, 'The Impact of the Mariel Boatlift on the Miami Labor Market', *Industrial and Labor Relations Review*, Vol. 43, No. 2, 1990, pp. 245–7; and Jennifer Hunt, 'The Impact of the 1962 Repatriates from

Algeria on the French Labor Market', *Industrial and Labor Relations Review*, Vol. 45, No. 3, 1992, pp. 556–72.

20 The figure was given by Michael Rogowski, President of the Federal Union of German Industry, cited on the SPD website (*www.spd.de*).

21 Glover et al., *Migration*, p. 37.

22 Bill Wells, *Inward Migration of Skilled Labour to the UK*, IPPR Discussion Paper (London: Institute for Public Policy Research, 2001).

23 Ibid.

24 Ignazio Visco, *Ageing Populations: Economic Issues and Policy Challenges*, Working Paper presented at the OECD Conference on Economic Policy for Ageing Societies (Paris: OECD, 2001), p. 2.

25 Jonathan Coppel, Jean-Christophe Dumont and Ignazio Visco, *Trends in Migration and Economic Consequences*, Economics Department Working Paper No. 284 (Paris: OECD, 2001), p. 20.

26 Cited in Commission of the European Communities, *Communication from the Commission to the Council and the European Parliament on a Community Immigration Policy* (COM (2000) 575 Final), p. 24.

27 Visco, *Ageing Populations*, p. 8.

28 UN Secretariat, 'Replacement Migration: Is it a Solution to Declining and Ageing Populations?' (ESA/P/WP.160), 2000, p. 3.

29 Visco, *Ageing Populations*, p. 13; OECD, *Maintaining Prosperity in an Ageing Society* (Paris: OECD, 1998).

30 For a discussion, see Janet Dobson et al., *International Migration and the UK: Recent Patterns and Trends*, RDS Occasional Paper No. 75 (London: Home Office 2001), pp. 274–5.

31 International Organization for Migration, 'Trafficking in Migrants', *Quarterly Bulletin* No. 21, Summer 2000.

32 Dobson et al., *International Migration and the UK*, p. 224.

33 Ibid., pp. 229–30.

34 Lavenex, 'Skilled Labor and European Immigration Policies', p. 12. In fact, schools had also been recruiting foreign teachers since the early 1990s. See Dobson et al., *International Migration and the UK*, p. 5.

35 'Skilled Labor and European Immigration Policies', p. 12.

36 Home Office, 'Secure Borders, Safe Havens: Integration with Diversity in Modern Britain' (2002), p. 11.

37 Department of Trade and Industry, 'Our Competitive Future: Building the Knowledge Economy', 1998 (available at *www.dti.gov.uk*).

38 Lavenex, 'Skilled Labor and European Immigration Policies', p. 13.

39 Home Office, 'Secure Borders, Safe Havens', p. 107.

40 Ibid., pp. 44–5.

41 *The Daily Telegraph*, 'Blunkett Shows Initiative', editorial, 8 February 2002.

42 Home Office, 'Building Trust and Confidence – Home Secretary Tackles Asylum Abuse and Increases Managed Economic Migration', Press Release, 7 October 2002.

43 Home Office, 'Bringing in the Skills and People Uur Businesses Need – New Managed Migration Boost', Press Release, 27 November 2002.

44 Home Office, 'Migrants Boost UK Labour Market', Press Release, 10 December 2002.

45 Home Office, 'Home Secretary to Launch Concerted Drive Against Illegal Immigration', News Release, 3 October 2001.

46 Home Office, 'Migrants Boost UK Labour Market'.

47 OECD SOPEMI, *Trends in International Migration* (Paris: OECD, 2001), p. 174.

48 Ibid.

49 Lavenex, 'Skilled Labor and European Immigration Policies', p. 10.

50 Ibid., pp. 20–21.

51 European Industrial Relations Observatory Online, 'Work permits for computer experts cause controversy', March 2000 (available at: *www.eiro.eurofound.ie*).

52 Migration und Bevölkerung, 'Deutschland/USA: Ausländische Arbeitskräfte für die Computerbranche', Newsletter, 16 March 2000 (see *www.demographie.de*). (Migration und Bevölkerung is an information centre sponsored by the German Federal Centre for Political Education.)

53 Independent Commission on Migration to Germany, *Structuring Immigration, Fostering Integration*, Berlin, 4 July 2001.

54 Schily often emphasized the social partners' support for the legislation as he defended the bill in parliament. See, for example, Bundestag debate of 1 March 2002, 'Rede des Bundesministers des Innern Otto Schily zum Entwurf eines Gesetzes zur Steuerung und Begrenzung der Zuwanderung und zur Regelung des Aufenthaltes und der Integration von Unionsbürgern und Ausländern' (available at *www.217.160.93.160/spd.schily/reden/reden_aa.htlm*).

55 In fact, the background to this rejection was complicated. Approval of the bill required a positive vote from the SPD–CDU coalition government of Brandenburg, but the coalition was openly split on its position. The SPD Minister President of Brandenburg voted in favour and the CDU interior minister voted against, prompting a heated constitutional debate as to whether the Brandenburg vote should be counted as valid (the German constitution requires that federal states vote *en bloc* in the Bundesrat). The president of the Bundesrat counted the vote as in favour, a decision which was subsequently overturned by a decision of the Constitutional Court in January 2003. The February 2003 *Länder* elections overturned the SPD–Green majority in the Bundesrat, making it highly unlikely that the bill could be passed in its current form.

56 Giovanna Zincone, 'Italy – Main Features of Italian Immigration Flows', paper presented at the German Marshall Fund of the United States meeting on 'The Transatlantic Dialogue on Refugee and Asylum Policies', 16–17 October 2001, p. 6.

57 This is the estimate of the Diocesan Caritas of Rome, cited in Ferruccio Pastore, 'Nationality Law and International Migration: The Italian Case,' in Randall Hansen and Patrick Weil (eds), *Towards a European Nationality: Citizenship, Immigration and Nationality Law in the EU* (Basingstoke: Palgrave, 2001), p. 104.

58 European Industrial Relations Observatory Online, 'Demand for Immigrant Workers Increases', November 2000 (available at *www.eiro.eurofound.ie*).

59 Ibid.

60 Pensioners even came onto the streets in protest at the proposed Bossi-Fini law in April 2002. See *Migration News*, Vol. 9, No. 5, May 2002.

61 OECD SOPEMI, *Trends in International Migration* (Paris: OECD, 1999), p. 163.

62 A poll by the research centre Censis found that 73 per cent of those surveyed agreed that foreigners were needed to do jobs that Italians did not want to do, and that 62 per cent did not believe that immigration caused unemployment. See *Migration News*, Vol. 8, No. 1, January 2001.

63 Alison Pargeter, *Italy and the Western Mediterranean*, Working Paper 26/01, ESRC 'One Europe or Several?' Programme, June 2001, p. 14.

64 *Migration News*, Vol. 9, No. 3, November 2002.

65 Pargeter, 'Italy and the Western Mediterranean', p. 6.

66 The figures are from a Censis poll, cited in *Migration News*, Vol. 8, No. 1, January 2001. These views are actually belied by the available statistics, which suggest that the proportion of non-EEA nationals in Italian prisons is less than in many other European countries. In 2000 it stood at 24.2 per cent, compared to over 45 per cent in Greece, more than 36 per cent in Belgium and around 34 per cent in Germany and Holland. Austria, France and Sweden also had higher proportions. See the statistics cited in Zincone, 'Italy – Main Features of Italian Immigration Flows', p. 7.

67 Francesco Speroni, cited in Luke Baker, 'Italians Pack Heat Against Immigrant Crime Wave', Reuters, 24 April 2002.

68 Ministero del Lavoro e delle Politiche Sociali, *Libro Bianco sul Mercato del Lavoro in Italia: Proposte per una Società Attiva e per un Lavoro di Qualità* (Rome, October 2001).

69 Pastore, 'Nationality Law and International Migration', p. 104.

70 Cited in Gavin Jones, 'The Trouble with a Long Coastline', *Financial Times*, 22 July 2002.

71 Ibid.

72 European Industrial Relations Observatory Online, 'New Legislation Regulates Immigration', September 2002 (available at *www.eiro.eurofound.ie*).

### 3 ASYLUM-SEEKERS AND ILLEGAL IMMIGRANTS

1 'Europe's Need for Immigrants', *The Economist*, 4 May 2000, available at *http://www.economist.com*.

2 Lavenex, 'Skilled Labor and European Immigration Policies'.

3 This point has been acknowledged by the European Commission. See Commission of the European Communities, *Communication from the Commission to the Council and the European Parliament on a Community Immigration Policy*, COM (2000) 757 Final, 22 November 2000, p. 25.

4 Although asylum-seekers and illegal immigrants represent separate categories of migrants, the two are often conflated in public debate. This is partly because many asylum-seekers enter west European states illegally, since there are limited options for legal entry. Thus the phenomenon of illegal migration flows encompasses both 'economic' migrants and genuine refugees. Moreover, many of those who apply for asylum are in fact would-be economic migrants, a problem which has generated the problem of asylum 'abuse' by non-genuine applicants. The overlap and difficulties in distinguishing between the two categories has led some researchers to define contemporary flows into western Europe as 'asylum migration', thereby merging the concepts of asylum-seekers and economic migration.

Because of this confusion between the two categories, popular resentment against migration is often targeted against asylum-seekers too.

5 Data kindly provided by the UNHCR Statistics Unit, Geneva.

6 Wolken, *Das Grundrecht auf Asyl*, p. 233.

7 Joppke, *Immigration and the Nation-state*, pp. 85–94.

8 Ibid., p. 134.

9 As the Home Office estimated in 1994, around 70 per cent of applicants actually originated from those entering legally as tourists or students or on business. *Migration News*, Vol. 3, No. 2, February 1996.

10 See, for example, Commission for Racial Equality, *Asylum-Seekers and Race Relations: The Commission for Racial Equality's View* (2000), available at *www.cre.gov.uk/misc/Asylnote.html*.

11 The Conservative Secretary of State for Social Security Peter Lilley, June 1996. See House of Commons, *Hansard Debates*, available at *www.parliament.the-stationery-office.co.uk*. For an analysis of these parliamentary debates on asylum, see Lena Jones, 'Immigration and Parliamentary Discourse in Great Britain: An Analysis of the Debates Related to the 1996 Asylum and Immigration Act', in Ruth Wodak and Teun A. van Dijk (eds), *Racism at the Top: Party Discourse on Ethnic Issues in Six European States* (Klagenfurt: Drava, 2000), pp. 283–310.

12 Financing for this comes from the European Refugee Fund, described in Chapter 5 of this book.

13 PLS Ramboll Management, *Country Profile: Italy* (Brussels: European Community, 2001), carried out on behalf of the European Commission Directorate-General Justice and Home Affairs.

14 Illegal migration is most commonly associated with clandestine border crossing or entry with forged documents, but the term also covers those who are illegally resident in a particular country, often through overstaying a tourist, student or business visa. A third type of illegality linked to migration is the act of taking employment without the necessary permission, referred to here as illegal employment.

15 There is an important definitional distinction between people-smuggling and people-trafficking. According to the European Commission (and following the definitions set out in the 2001 UN Convention against Transnational Organized Crime and its protocols on smuggling and trafficking), 'smuggling is connected with the support of an illegal border crossing and illegal entry. Smuggling, therefore, always has a transnational element. This is not necessarily the case with trafficking, where the key element is the exploitative purpose. Trafficking involves the intent to exploit a person, in principal independent from the question as to how the victim comes to the location where the exploitation takes place.' See Commission of the European Communities, *Communication from the Commission to the Council and the European Parliament on a Common Policy on Illegal Immigration*, COM(2001) 672 Final, 15 November 2001, p. 21.

16 Kyle and Koslowski, 'Introduction', in Kyle and Koslowski (eds), *Global Human Smuggling*, p. 4.

17 Zincone, 'Italy – Main Features of Italian Immigration Flows', p. 1.

18 Kyle and Kowlowski, 'Introduction', pp. 3–4.

19 Italy had in fact signed the Schengen Agreement in 1990, but it did not remove

immigration controls for those travelling by air from other Schengen countries until 1997, and it removed controls for those arriving by land or sea only in 1998.

20 On this theme, see Faist, 'How to Define a Foreigner?', in Baldwin-Edwards and Schain (eds), *The Politics of Immigration in Western Europe*, pp. 50–71.

21 Home Office, 'Secure Borders, Safe Havens: Integration with Diversity in Modern Britain', *White Paper* (2002), p. 76.

22 Exceptions include research by Anita Böcker and Tetty Havinga, 'Asylum Migration to the European Union: Patterns of Origin and Destination', report prepared for the European Commission (1997); and Vaughan Robinson and Jeremy Segrott, 'Understanding the Decision-making of Asylum-seekers', Home Office Research Study No. 243 (London: Home Office, 2002).

23 Robinson and Segrott, ibid., found that the main factors influencing choice of country (for those in a position to choose at all) were 'whether they had relatives or friends here; their belief that the UK is a safe, tolerant and democratic country; previous links between their own country and the UK including colonialism; and their ability to speak English or desire to learn it'. These factors emerged as more important than knowledge of the British asylum system.

24 Home Office Immigration and Nationality Directorate, 'Trust and Confidence in our Nationality, Immigration and Asylum System – Bill Published', 12 April 2002 (available at *www.ind.homeoffice.gov.uk*).

25 Independent Commission on Migration to Germany, *Structuring Immigration, Fostering Integration*, Berlin, 4 July 2000, p. 95.

26 Ibid., p. 117.

27 The perceived need to keep humanitarian and economic aspects of migration reform separate has also been endorsed by a number of economists commenting on the law. See, for example, Lüder Gerken, Volker Rieble and Thomas Straubhaar, *Mehr Mut zur Zuwanderung: Der arbeitsmarktpolitische Teil des geplanten Zuwanderungsgesetzes verfehlt sein eigenes Ziel* [*A Bolder Approach to Migration. The Labour Market Policy Aspect of the Proposed Migration Law Misses its Own Target*] (Frankfurter Institut Stiftung Marktwirtschaft und Politik, 2002).

28 German asylum law distinguishes between refugees granted status under the 1951 Geneva Convention (see Chapter 1), and 'constitutional' refugees granted status under German Basic Law. As shown in Chapter 1, each embraces a slightly different definition of 'refugee'.

29 Die Grünen, 'Beschluss Einwanderungspolitik', 23. ordentlicher Parteirat, Berlin, 3 September 2001.

30 The extension applied to those with refugee status under the Geneva Convention, not to those under the German constitution.

31 See, for example, the presentation of the new bill on the SPD website (*www.spd.de*).

32 Vera Gaserow, 'Bundesrat lehnt das Zuwanderungsgesetz ab', *Frankfurter Rundschau*, 21 December 2001.

33 This decision was subsequently overturned by the constitutional court, as explained in Chapter 2.

34 See the House of Commons debate on the Nationality, Immigration and Asylum Bill from 24 April 2002, in *Hansard Debates*, available at *http://www.parliament. the-stationery-office.co.uk*.

35 Home Office, 'Secure Borders, Safe Havens'.

36 Ibid., pp. 11, 75 and 48.

37 Home Office, 'Home Secretary to Launch Concerted Drive against Illegal Immigration', News Release, 3 October 2001.

38 Immigration and Nationality Directorate, Home Office, Press Release, 12 April 2002.

39 Home Office Immigration and Nationality Directorate, 'Trust and Confidence in our Nationality, Immigration and Asylum System – Bill Published', Press Release, 24 April 2002. The measure was on the exclusion of those who had been sentenced to two or more years in prison.

40 House of Commons debate on the Nationality, Immigration and Asylum Bill from 24 April 2002, in *Hansard Debates*, available at *www.parliament.the-stationery-office.co.uk*.

## 4 LABOUR MIGRATION, INTEGRATION AND DIVERSITY

1 For a classic statement of this liberal concept of 'overlapping consensus', see John Rawls, *Political Liberalism* (New York: Columbia University Press, 1993), pp. 150–54.

2 However, a concept of multiculturalism has also been embraced by states with a stronger social democratic model, notably Sweden and the Netherlands.

3 Christina Boswell, 'European Values and the Asylum Crisis', *International Affairs*, Vol. 76, No. 3 October 2000, pp. 537–57, at p. 554.

4 Adrian Favell picks up on this Hobbesian element in British thinking on race relations. See Favell, *Philosophies of Integration*, pp. 136–8.

5 Ibid., pp. 116–17.

6 Interestingly, this is not a categorization shared by most continental European states. Thus in France the discourse concentrates on problems of religious and cultural difference; in the Netherlands it focuses on the social behaviour of different migrant groups. See Frank Bovenkerk, Robert Miles and Gilles Verbunt, 'Racism, Migration and the State in Western Europe: A Case for Comparative Analysis', *International Sociology*, Vol. 5, No. 4, December 1990, p. 493.

7 Muhammad Anwar, Patrick Roach and Ranjit Sondhi, 'Introduction', in Anwar, Roach and Sondhi (eds), *From Legislation to Integration? Race Relations in Britain* (Basingstoke: Macmillan, 2000), pp. 1–23.

8 Cited in Joppke, *Immigration and the Nation-state*, p. 226.

9 Rogers Brubaker, *Citizenship and Nationhood in France and Germany* (Cambridge, MA: Harvard University Press, 1992).

10 Joppke, *Immigration and the Nation-state*, p. 211.

11 Jasmin Nuhoglu Soysal, *Limits of Citizenship: Migrants and Postnational Membership in Europe* (Chicago and London: University of Chicago Press, 1994), pp. 108 and 78.

12 Hammar, *European Immigration*.

13 Cited in Joppke, *Immigration and the Nation-state*, p. 188.

14 See, for example, Bernhard Santel, 'Ein gradueller, kein kategorischer Unterschied: Einwanderungs- und Integrationspolitk in Deutschland und den Vereinigten

Staaten', in Uwe Hunger, Karin Meendermann, Bernhard Santel and Richard Woyke (eds), *Migration in erklärten und 'unerklärten' Einwanderungsländern – Analyse und Vergleich* (Münster: Lit Verlag, 2001), pp. 80–81.

15 For a strong statement of this thesis, see Joppke, *Immigration and the Nation-state*, p. 188.

16 Ibid., p. 202.

17 Ellie Vasta, 'Rights and Racism in a New Country of Immigration: The Italian Case', in John Solomos and Jon Wrench (eds), *Racism and Migration in Western Europe* (Oxford: Berg, 1993), p. 98.

18 Ibid., pp. 91–2.

19 Paul Statham, *The Political Construction of Immigration in Italy: Opportunities, Mobilisation and Outcomes* (Berlin: Wissenschaftszentrum Berlin für Soziale Forschung, 1998), p. 21.

20 Anna Triandafyllidou, 'Nation and Immigration', p. 70.

21 Ibid., pp. 82–3.

22 Statham, *The Political Construction of Immigration in Italy*, pp. 42–3.

23 James Blitz, 'Berlusconi's immigration policy rings alarm bells', *Financial Times*, 1 April 2000.

24 Zincone, 'Immigration to Italy', in F. Heckmann and W. Bosswick (eds), *Migration Policies: A Comparative Perspective* (Stuttgart: Enke, 1995), p. 152.

25 Statham, *The Political Construction of Immigration in Italy*, p. 28.

26 See Zincone, 'Italy – Main Features of Italian Immigration Flows'. A number of the provisions in the legislation have since been rescinded: social assistance has now been denied to immigrants and maternity allowance has been limited.

27 Cited in Pastore, 'Nationality Law and International Migration', p. 106.

28 Vasta, 'Rights and Racism in a New Country of Immigration', p. 98.

29 Watts, *Immigration Policy and the Challenge of Globalization*, p. 12.

30 Zincone, 'Immigration to Italy', pp. 150–51.

31 The EU Council of Ministers adopted two directives in June 2000 on racial discrimination and discrimination in the workplace, which member states were bound to incorporate into law by July 2003.

32 On the problems of segregation and 'ghettoization' in German states, see contributions in Heinz Fassmann, Josef Kohlbacher and Ursula Reeger (eds), *Zuwanderung und Segregation: Europäische Metropolen im Vergleich* (Klagenfurt: Drava, 2002).

33 Wolfgang Seifert, 'Social and Economic Integration of Foreigners in Germany', in Peter Schuck and Rainer Münz (eds), *Paths to Inclusion: The Integration of Migrants in the UK and Germany* (Oxford and New York: Berghahn Books, 1998), p. 98.

34 Friedrich Heckmann, 'Is there a Migration Policy in Germany?', in F. Heckmann and W. Bosswick (eds), *Migration Policies: A Comparative Perspective* (Stuttgart: Enke, 1995), p. 170.

35 See Friedrich Merz, 'Einwanderung und Identität', *Die Welt*, 25 October 2000.

36 Bundeszentrale für politische Bildung, 'Was ist Integration?', available at *http://www.bpb.de/zuwanderung/synopse/body-integration.htlm*.

37 Independent Commission on Migration to Germany, *Structuring Immigration, Fostering Integration*, Berlin, 4 July 2000, p. 246.

38 Ibid., p. 229.

39 Willian Macpherson, *The Stephen Lawrence Inquiry*, February 1999, available at *www.archive.official-documents.co.uk*.

40 Runnymede Trust, *The Future of Multi-Ethnic Britain* (London: Profile Books, 2000).

41 Bradford Race Review, *Community Pride, Not Prejudice: Making Diversity Work in Bradford* (2001), available at *www.bradford.gov.uk*.

42 Philip Lewis, *Islamic Britain: Religion, Politics and Identity among British Muslims* (London and New York: Tauris, 2nd edn, 2002), p. 217.

43 Ibid., p. 221.

44 See, for example, remarks by the Liberal Democrat leader, Charles Kennedy, reported in BBC News, 'Immigrants "should try to feel British"', 9 December 2001, available at *www.news.bbc.co.uk*.

45 Beck, *Risk Society*, p. 49.

46 Ibid., p. 75.

47 Etienne Balibar, 'Racism and Crisis', in Etienne Balibar and Immanuel Wallerstein (eds), *Race, Nation and Class* (London and New York: Verso, 1991), p. 219.

48 Stephen Castles, 'Migrations and Minorities in Europe – Perspectives for the 1990s: Eleven Hypotheses', in John Solomos and Jon Wrench (eds), *Racism and Migration in Western Europe* (Oxford: Berg, 1993), p. 28.

49 CDU–CSU, 'Stellungnahme der Union zum Bericht der Regierungskommission zur Zuwanderungspolitik', Press Conference, Berlin, 5 July 2001.

50 The Fortuyn List was a populist, anti-immigration political party founded in the Netherlands in February 2002 by the controversial politician Pim Fortuyn. Fortuyn was notorious for his outspoken and often extreme views on migration and refugee issues. On 6 May, a week before the Dutch general elections, he was shot dead by a lone gunman. Fortuyn's death prompted a huge and unexpected surge in popular sympathy for the politician and his views. It also contributed to the electoral breakthrough of the Fortuyn List in the subsequent elections, with the party – under new leadership – securing the second highest number of seats in the parliament and becoming a coalition partner in the new government.

51 Kate Connolly, 'Polls show strong German opposition to immigrants. Survey strengthens hand of rightwing candidate for chancellor', *The Guardian*, 3 May 2002.

52 Kurt Biedenkopf, speech in the Bundesrat debate on the Migration Law, 22 March 2002, extract from the stenographic report of the 774th sitting.

53 Peter Müller, 'Von der Einwanderungskontrolle zum Zuwanderungsmanagement: Plädoyer für ein nationales Programm der Zuwanderungspolitik in Deutschland', CDU-Bundesgeschäftsstelle, available at *www.cdu.de*.

## 5 THE INTERNATIONAL CONTEXT

1 The precise criteria are more complex, structured according to a hierarchy of conditions in descending order of importance. First, if the applicant has close family members who have already filed an asylum application in another member state, the state hosting the family members assumes responsibility. Secondly, member states where the applicant has been granted a valid residence permit, or a

valid visa, assume responsibility. In cases where none of these conditions apply, the state through which an applicant first entered the EU illegally assumes responsibility, unless the applicant has been residing in another state for over six months, in which case that country is responsible.

2 Council of the European Union, General Secretariat DGH, 'EU Schengen Catalogue: External Borders Control, Removal and Readmission'.

3 Grabbe, 'The Sharp Edges of Europe', pp. 519–36.

4 *Presidency Conclusions*, Seville European Council (SN/200/1/02/REV 1), 21–22 June 2002.

5 Estimates of illegal migration flows are, of course, extremely difficult to derive. The most commonly cited estimate is Europol's figure of annual illegal flows into the EU, which puts the figure at 500,000 per year. But this must be treated as a very rough estimate. On the increase in illegal flows, see, for example, the European Union Council, *Strategy Paper on Immigration and Asylum Policy*, presented to the K4 Committee, Brussels (LIMITE CK4 27 ASIM 170), available at *www.proasyl.de*, 1 July 1998.

6 It should be noted that for many countries it is more common for immigrants to become illegal residents through overstaying temporary visas than through entering illegally. This is certainly the case for the UK.

7 See Commission of the European Communities, *Communication from the Commission to the Council and the European Parliament on a Common Policy on Illegal Immigration*, COM (2001) 672 Final, 15 November 2001, pp. 17–18.

8 Ibid., p. 9.

9 *Presidency Conclusions*, para. 33.

10 Ibid., paras 33 and 36.

11 Christina Boswell, 'The "External Dimension" of EU Immigration and Asylum Policy', *International Affairs*, Vol. 79, No. 3, May 2003, pp. 619–38.

12 Christina Boswell, *Spreading the Costs of Asylum-seekers: A Critical Assessment of Dispersal Policies in Germany and the UK*, Anglo-German Foundation Report (London: AGF, 2001). It should be noted, however, that under the German system the sole criterion for distribution is population – factors such as GDP or size of territory are not taken into account.

13 Council of the European Union, *Council Resolution on Burden-sharing with Regard to the Admission and Residence of Displaced Persons on a Temporary Basis* (ASIM 204), 25 September 1995.

14 Treaty of Amsterdam, Article 63.

15 UNHCR figures, cited in Joanne van Selm (ed.), *Kosovo's Refugees in the European Union* (London: Pinter Publishers, 2000), p. 224.

16 Treaty of Amsterdam, Article 63.

17 In the sphere of migration, the so-called 'open coordination method' is a tool for harmonizing EU migration policies, involving 'the identification and development of common objectives' and guidelines, which then serve as a benchmark for coordinating national policies and assessing progress towards the stated common goals. See Commission of the European Communities, *Communication from the Commission to the Council and the European Parliament on an Open Method of Coordination for the Community Immigration Policy*, COM (2001) 387 Final, Brussels, 11 July 2001.

18 See, for example, Ferruccio Pastore, 'Why did the Communitarization of Immigration and Asylum Policies Almost Fail and How Should We Revive It?', Special Issue, *Migraction Europa* (Rome: CeSPI, 2002).

19 Robinson and Segrott, 'Understanding the Decision-making of Asylum-seekers'.

20 See, for example, Eiko Thielemann, 'Does Policy Harmonisation Work? The EU's Role in Regulating Migration Flows', paper prepared for the 8th European Union Studies Association Biennial International Conference, Nashville, Tennessee 27–29 March 2003. In fact, despite Home Secretary David Blunkett's continued support for this process, there are increasing doubts even within the Home Office as to whether EU harmonization will really reduce the proportion of asylum-seekers entering the UK.

21 See, for example, Birgit Jennen, Tina Stadlmayer and Karin Nink, 'Berlin blockiert EU-Einwanderungspolitik', *Financial Times Deutschland*, 1 December 2000.

22 For a discussion of these conflicting tendencies, see Anna Triandafyllidou, 'Migration, Identity and European Integration in the Italian Debate', paper prepared for the IDNET–OSU Conference on 'Europeanisation and Multiple Identities', Florence, 9–10 June 2000, p. 15.

23 Sadruddin Aga Khan, 'Study on Human Rights and Massive Exoduses', UN Commission on Human Rights, 38th Session, E/CN.4/1503, 1981.

24 See in particular Aristide R. Zolberg, Astri Suhrke and Sergio Aguayo, *Escape from Violence: Conflict and the Refugee Crisis in the Developing World: Beyond Progress and Development* (Oxford and New York: Oxford University Press, 1989).

25 Philip L. Martin, *Trade and Migration: NAFTA and Agriculture* (Washington, DC: Institute for International Economics, 1993).

26 See, for example, Ninna Nyberg-Sorensen, Nicholas Van Hear and Poul Engberg-Pedersen, 'The Migration–Development Nexus: Policy Study' (Copenhagen: Centre for Development Research, 2002).

27 Christina Boswell, 'Preventing the Causes of Migration and Refugee Flows: Towards an EU Policy Framework', *New Issues in Refugee Research* (Geneva: UNHCR, December 2002).

28 Research shows that military intervention is one of the major causes of displacement. See Susanne Schmeidl, 'Conflict and Forced Migration: A Qualitative Review, 1964–1995', in Aristide R. Zolberg and Peter Benda (eds), *Global Migrants, Global Refugees: Problems and Solutions* (Oxford and New York: Berghahn Books, 2001), pp. 62–94.

29 See, for example, House of Commons Select Committee on European Communities, Nineteenth Report, *Prospects for the Tampere Special European Council*, 27 July 1999, available at *www. Parliament.the-stationery-office.co.uk*.

30 High Level Working Group on Asylum and Migration, *Final Report of the High Level Working Group on Asylum and Migration* 11281/99 (Presse 288-G), 4 December 1999.

31 Ibid.

32 Interviews with officials in DGs JHA and External Relations, March and October 2002. On the Commission's approach, see Commission of the European Communities, *Communication from the Commission to the Council and the European Parliament on Integrating Migration Issues in the EU's Relations with Third Countries*, COM (2002) 703 Final, 3 December 2002.

33 Yves Lernout, 'La Question de la Migration dans le Processus de Barcelone', European Commission DG External Relations, October 2002.

34 Partenariat Euro-Med, *Maroc: Document de Stratégie 2002–2006 et Programme Indicatif National 2002–2004*, 6 December 2001, p. 25 (available at *www.europa. eu.int/comm/external_relations*).

35 Secretariat of the Inter-governmental Consultations on Asylum, Refugee and Migration Policies in Europe, North America and Australia, *Working Paper on Reception in the Region of Origin* (Geneva: IGC, 1994).

36 Noll, Fagerlund and Liebaut, *Study on the Feasibiliy of Processing Asylum Claims Outside the EU.*

# References

Anwar, Muhammad, Patrick Roach and Ranjit Sondhi, 'Introduction', in Anwar, Roach and Sondhi (eds), *From Legislation to Integration? Race Relations in Britain* (Basingstoke: Macmillan, 2000), pp. 1–23.

Bade, Klaus J., *Europa in Bewegung: Migration vom späten 18. Jahrhundert bis zur Gegenwart* (Munich: Verlag C. H. Beck, 2000).

Balibar, Etienne, 'Racism and Crisis', in Etienne Balibar and Immanuel Wallerstein (eds), *Race, Nation and Class* (London and New York: Verso, 1991), pp. 217–27.

Beck, Ulrich, *Risk Society: Towards a New Modernity* (London: Sage, 1992).

Böcker, Anita and Tetty Havinga, 'Asylum Migration to the European Union: Patterns of Origin and Destination', report prepared for the European Commission, (1997).

Boswell, Christina, 'European Values and the Asylum Crisis', *International Affairs*, Vol. 76, No. 3, October 2000, pp. 537–57.

Boswell, Christina, *EU Enlargement: What are the Prospects for East–West Migration?*, European Programme Working Paper (London: Royal Institute of International Affairs, November 2000).

Boswell, Christina, *Spreading the Costs of Asylum Seekers: A Critical Assessment of Dispersal Policies in Germany and the UK*, Anglo-German Foundation Report (London: AGF, 2001).

Boswell, Christina, 'Preventing the Causes of Migration and Refugee Flows: Towards an EU Policy Framework', *New Issues in Refugee Research* (Geneva: UNHCR, December 2002).

Boswell, Christina, 'The "External Dimension" of EU Immigration and Asylum Policy', *International Affairs*, Vol. 79, No. 3, May 2003, pp. 619–38.

Bovenkerk, Frank, Robert Miles and Gilles Verbunt, 'Racism, Migration and the State in Western Europe: A Case for Comparative Analysis', *International Sociology*, Vol. 5, No. 4, December 1990, pp. 475–90.

Brubaker, Rogers, *Citizenship and Nationhood in France and Germany* (Cambridge, MA: Harvard University Press, 1992).

Card, David, 'The Impact of the Mariel Boatlift on the Miami Labor Market', *Industrial and Labor Relations Review*, Vol. 43, No. 2, 1990, pp. 245–7.

Castells, Manuel, 'Information Technology and Global Capitalism', in Will Hutton and Anthony Giddens (eds), *Global Capitalism* (New York: The New Press, 2000), pp. 52–74.

Castles, Stephen, 'Migrations and Minorities in Europe – Perspectives for the 1990s: Eleven Hypotheses', in John Solomos and Jon Wrench (eds), *Racism and Migration in Western Europe* (Oxford: Berg, 1993), pp. 17–34.

Castles, Stephen, 'The Racisms of Globalization', in Stephen Castles (ed.), *Ethnicity and Globalization* (London: Sage, 2000), pp. 163–86.

Castles, Stephen and Alastair Davidson, *Citizenship and Migration: Globalization and the Politics of Belonging* (New York: Routledge, 2000).

Collinson, Sarah, *Europe and International Migration* (London: Royal Institute of International Affairs/Pinter Publishers, 2nd edn, 1994).

Coppel, Jonathan, Jean-Christophe Dumont and Ignazio Visco, *Trends in Migration and Economic Consequences*, Economics Department Working Paper No. 284 (Paris: OECD, 2001).

Cornelius, Wayne A., Philip L. Martin and James F. Hollifield (eds), *Controlling Migration: A Global Perspective* (Stanford, CA: Stanford University Press, 1992).

Dittgen, Herbert, 'Immigration Control: Some Observations on National Traditions, Internal and External Controls and Policy Paradigms', in Axel Schulte and Dietrich Thränhardt (eds), *International Migration and Liberal Democracies* (Münster: Lit Verlag, 1999), pp. 77–86.

Dobson, Janet, et al., *International Migration and the UK: Recent Patterns and Trends*, RDS Occasional Paper No. 75 (London: Home Office, 2001).

Faist, Thomas, 'How to Define a Foreigner? The Symbolic Politics of Immigration in German Partisan Discourse, 1978–1992', in Martin Baldwin-Edwards and Martin A. Schain (eds), *The Politics of Immigration in Western Europe* (Ilford: Frank Cass, 1994), pp. 50–71.

Faist, Thomas, *The Volume and Dynamics of International Migration and Trans-national Social Spaces* (Oxford: Clarendon Press, 2000).

Fassmann, Heinz and Rainer Münz (eds), *European Migration in the Late Twentieth Century* (Laxenburg: International Institute for Applied Systems Analysis, 1994).

Fassmann, Heinz, Josef Kohlbacher and Ursula Reeger (eds), *Zuwanderung und Segregation: Europäische Metropolen im Vergleich* (Klagenfurt: Drava, 2002).

Favell, Adrian, *Philosophies of Integration: Immigration and the Idea of Citizenship in France and Britain* (London: Macmillan Press, 2nd edn, 2001).

Freeman, Gary P., *Immigrant Labor and Racial Conflict in Industrial Societies: The French and British Experience 1945–1975* (Princeton, NJ: Princeton University Press, 1979).

Freeman, Gary P., 'Modes of Immigration Politics in Liberal Democratic States', *International Migration Review*, Vol. 29, No. 4, 1995, pp. 881–902.

Geddes, Andrew and Adrian Favell (eds), *The Politics of Belonging: Migrants and Minorities in Contemporary Europe* (Aldershot: Ashgate, 1999).

Gerken, Lüder, Volker Rieble and Thomas Straubhaar, *Mehr Mut zur Zuwanderung: Der arbeitsmarktpolitische Teil des geplanten Zuwanderungsgesetzes verfehlt sein eigenes Ziel*, Frankfurter Institut Stiftung Marktwirtschaft und Politik, 2002.

Ghosh, Bimal, *Gains from Global Linkages: Trade in Services and Movements of Persons* (Basingstoke: Macmillan in association with IOM, 1997).

Giddens, Anthony and Will Hutton, 'In Conversation', in Will Hutton and

Anthony Giddens (eds), *On the Edge: Living with Global Capitalism* (London: Vintage, 2001), pp. 1–52.

Glover, Stephen, et al., *Migration: An Economic and Social Analysis*, RDS Occasional Paper No. 67 (London: Home Office, 2001).

Grabbe, Heather, 'The Sharp Edges of Europe: Extending Schengen Eastwards', *International Affairs*, Vol. 76, No. 3, July 2000, pp. 519–36.

Hammar, Tomas, *European Immigration Policy* (Cambridge: Cambridge University Press, 1985).

Hathaway, James C., *The Law of Refugee Status* (Toronto and Vancouver: Butterworths, 1991).

Heckmann, Friedrich, 'Is there a Migration Policy in Germany?', in F. Heckmann and W. Bosswick (eds), *Migration Policies: A Comparative Perspective* (Stuttgart: Enke, 1995), pp. 157–70.

Heisler, Martin O. and Zig Layton-Henry, 'Migration and the Links between Social and Societal Security', in Ole Weaver, Barry Buzan, Morten Kelstrup and Pierre Lemaire (eds), *Identity, Migration and the New Security Agenda in Europe* (London: Pinter Publishers, 1993), pp. 148–66.

Held, David, 'Democracy and Globalization', in Daniele Archibugi, David Held and Martin Köhler (eds), *Re-imagining Political Community: Studies in Cosmopolitan Democracy* (Cambridge: Polity, 1998), pp. 11–27.

Hennessey, Peter, *Never Again: Britain 1945–1951* (London: Vintage, 1993).

Herbert, Ulrich, *Geschichte der Ausländerpolitik in Deutschland: Saisonarbeiter, Zwangsarbeiter, Gastarbeiter, Flüchtlinge* (Munich: Verlag C. H. Beck, 2001).

Hollifield, James F., 'Ideas, Institutions, and Civil Society: On the Limits of Immigration Control in France', in Grete Brochmann and Tomas Hammar (eds), *Mechanisms of Immigration Control: A Comparative Analysis of European Regulation Policies* (Oxford and New York: Berg, 1999), pp. 59–95.

Hollifield, James F., 'Immigration and Republicanism in France: The Hidden Consensus', in Wayne A. Cornelius, Philip L. Martin and James F. Hollifield (eds), *Controlling Migration: A Global Perspective* (Stanford, CA: Stanford University Press, 1992), pp. 143–75.

Hollifield, James F., *Immigrants, Markets and States: The Political Economy of Postwar Europe* (Cambridge, MA: Harvard University Press, 1992).

Hunt, Jennifer, 'The Impact of the 1962 Repatriates from Algeria on the French Labor Market', *Industrial and Labor Relations Review*, Vol. 45, No. 3, 1992, pp. 556–72.

Jones, Lena, 'Immigration and Parliamentary Discourse in Great Britain: An Analysis of the Debates Related to the 1996 Asylum and Immigration Act', in Ruth Wodak and Teun A. van Dijk (eds), *Racism at the Top: Party Discourse on Ethnic Issues in Six European States* (Klagenfurt: Drava, 2000), pp. 283–310.

Joppke, Christian, *Immigration and the Nation-state: The United States, Germany and Great Britain* (Oxford and New York: Oxford University Press, 1999).

Koopmans, Ruud and Paul Statham, 'Migration and Ethnic Relations as a Field of Political Contention: An Opportunity Structure Approach', in Ruud Koopmans and Paul Statham (eds), *Challenging Immigration and Ethnic Relations Politics: Comparative European Perspectives* (Oxford and New York: Oxford University Press, 2000), pp. 13–56.

Kushner, Tony and Katharine Knox, *Refugees in an Age of Genocide* (London and Portland, OR: Frank Cass, 1999).

Kyle, David and Rey Koslowski, 'Introduction', in David Kyle and Rey Koslowski (eds), *Global Human Smuggling: Comparative Perspectives* (Baltimore and London: Johns Hopkins University Press, 2001), pp. 1–25.

Lavenex, Sandra, *The Europeanisation of Refugee Policies: Between Human Rights and Internal Security* (Aldershot, Hants: Ashgate, 2001).

Lavenex, Sandra, 'Skilled Labor and European Immigration Policies: A Shift of Paradigms?', paper presented at the International Studies Association annual meeting, New Orleans, 23–27 March 2002.

Lavenex, Sandra, 'Labour Mobility in the General Agreement on Trade in Services (GATS) – Background Paper', PEMINT Working Paper 1/2002 (2002).

Layton-Henry, Zig, *The Politics of Immigration: 'Race' and 'Race' Relations in Post-War Britain* (Oxford: Blackwell, 1992).

Lernout, Yves, 'La Question de la Migration dans le Processus de Barcelone', European Commission DG External Relations, October 2002.

Lewis, Philip, *Islamic Britain: Religion, Politics and Identity among British Muslims* (London and New York: Tauris, 2nd edn, 2002)

Lin, Lin Leam, 'International Labour Movements: A Perspective on Economic Exchanges and Flows', in Mary M. Kritz, Lin Leam Lin and Hania Zlotnik (eds), *International Migration Systems – A Global Approach* (Oxford and New York: Oxford University Press, 1992), pp. 133–49.

Macpherson, William, *The Stephen Lawrence Inquiry*, February 1999 (available at *www.archive.official–documents.co.uk*).

Martin, Philip L., *Trade and Migration: NAFTA and Agriculture* (Washington, DC: Institute for International Economics, 1993).

Noll, Gregor, Jessica Fagerlund and Fabrice Liebaut, *Study on the Feasibility of Processing Asylum Claims Outside the EU against the Background of the Common European Asylum System and the Goal of a Common Asylum Procedure*, Final Report (Brussels: European Community, 2002).

Nyberg-Sorensen, Ninna, Nicholas Van Hear and Poul Engberg-Pedersen, 'The Migration–Development Nexus: Policy Study' (Copenhagen: Centre for Development Research, 2002).

OECD, *Maintaining Prosperity in an Ageing Society* (Paris: OECD, 1998).

OECD SOPEMI, *Trends in International Migration* (Paris: OECD, 1999, 2001).

Overbeek, Henk, *Globalization and Governance: Contradictions of Neo–Liberal Migration Management*, HWWA Discussion Paper 174 (Hamburg: Hamburg Institute of International Economics, 2002).

Pargeter, Alison, *Italy and the Western Mediterranean*, Working Paper 26/01, ESRC 'One Europe or Several?' Programme, June 2001.

Pastore, Ferruccio, 'Nationality Law and International Migration: The Italian Case', in Randall Hansen and Patrick Weil (eds), *Towards a European Nationality: Citizenship, Immigration and Nationality Law in the EU* (Basingstoke: Palgrave, 2001), pp. 95–117.

Pastore, Ferruccio, 'Why did the Communitarization of Immigration and Asylum Policies Almost Fail and How Should We Revive It?', Special Issue, *Migraction Europa* (Rome: CeSPI, 2002).

# References

Rawls, John, *Political Liberalism* (New York: Columbia University Press, 1993).

Robinson, Vaughan and Jeremy Segrott, 'Understanding the Decision-making of Asylum-seekers', Home Office Research Study No. 243 (London: Home Office, 2002).

Runnymede Trust, *The Future of Multi-Ethnic Britain* (London: Profile Books, 2000).

Santel, Bernhard, 'Ein gradueller, kein kategorischer Unterschied: Einwanderungs- und Integrationspolitik in Deutschland und den Vereinigten Staaten', in Uwe Hunger, Karin Meendermann, Bernhard Santel and Richard Woyke (eds), *Migration in erklärten und 'unerklärten' Einwanderungsländern – Analyse und Vergleich* (Münster: Lit Verlag, 2001), pp. 65–88.

Sassen, Saskia, *The Mobility of Labor and Capital: A Study in International Investment and Labor Flow* (Cambridge and New York: Cambridge University Press, 1988).

Sassen, Saskia, *Losing Control? Sovereignty in an Age of Globalization* (New York: Columbia University Press, 1996).

Sassen, Saskia, *Guests and Aliens* (New York: The New Press, 1999).

Schmeidl, Susanne, 'Conflict and Forced Migration: A Qualitative Review, 1964–1995', in Aristide R. Zolberg and Peter Benda (eds), *Global Migrants, Global Refugees: Problems and Solutions* (Oxford and New York: Berghahn Books, 2001), pp. 62–94.

Secretariat of the Inter-governmental Consultations on Asylum, Refugee and Migration Policies in Europe, North America and Australia, *Working Paper on Reception in the Region of Origin* (Geneva: IGC, 1994).

Seifert, Wolfgang, 'Social and Economic Integration of Foreigners in Germany', in Peter Schuck and Rainer Münz (eds), *Paths to Inclusion: The Integration of Migrants in the UK and Germany* (Oxford and New York: Berghahn Books, 1998), pp. 83–113.

Soysal, Jasmin Nuhoglu, *Limits of Citizenship: Migrants and Postnational Membership in Europe* (Chicago and London: University of Chicago Press, 1994).

Stalker, Peter, *Workers without Frontiers: The Impact of Globalization on International Migration* (Boulder, CO and London: Lynne Rienner, 2000).

Statham, Paul, *The Political Construction of Immigration in Italy: Opportunities, Mobilisation and Outcomes* (Berlin: Wissenschaftszentrum Berlin für Soziale Forschung, 1998).

Straubhaar, Thomas, *Migration im 21. Jahrhundert: Von der Bedrohung zur Rettung sozialer Marktwirtschaften?* (Tübingen: Mohr Siebeck, 2002).

Suárez–Orozco, Marcelo M., 'Anxious Neighbors: Belgium and its Immigrant Minorities', in Wayne A. Cornelius, Philip L. Martin and James F. Hollifield (eds), *Controlling Migration: A Global Perspective* (Stanford, CA: Stanford University Press, 1992), pp. 237–68.

Thielemann, Eiko, 'Does Policy Harmonisation Work? The EU's Role in Regulating Migration Flows', paper prepared for the 8th European Union Studies Association Biennial International Conference, Nashville, Tennessee, 27–29 March 2003.

Triandafyllidou, Anna , 'Nation and Immigration: A Study of the Italian Press Discourse', *Social Identities*, Vol. 5, No. 1, 1999, pp. 65–88.

Triandafyllidou, Anna, 'Migration, Identity and European Integration in the Italian

Debate'. paper prepared for the IDNET–OSU Conference on 'Europeanisation and Mutiple Identities', Florence, 9–10 June 2000.

Triandafyllidou, Anna, *Immigrants and National Identity in Europe* (London: Routledge, 2001).

UN Secretariat, 'Replacement Migration: Is It a Solution to Declining and Ageing Populations?' (ESA/P/WP.160), 2000.

Van Selm, Joanne (ed.), *Kosovo's Refugees in the European Union* (London: Pinter Publishers, 2000).

Vasta, Ellie, 'Rights and Racism in a New Country of Immigration: The Italian Case', in John Solomos and Jon Wrench (eds), *Racism and Migration in Western Europe* (Oxford: Berg, 1993), pp. 83–98.

Veugelers, John W. P., 'Recent Immigration Politics in Italy: A Short Story', in Martin Baldwin-Edwards and Martin A. Schain (eds), *The Politics of Immigration in Western Europe* (Ilford: Frank Cass, 1994), pp. 33–49.

Visco, Ignazio, *Ageing Populations: Economic Issues and Policy Challenges*, Working Paper presented at the OECD Conference on 'Economic Policy for Ageing Societies', OECD, Paris, 2001.

Watts, Julie R., *Immigration Policy and the Challenge of Globalization: Unions and Employers in Unlikely Alliance* (Ithaca, NY and London: ILR Press, 2002).

Weis, Paul, *The Refugee Convention, 1951: The Travaux Préparatoires Analysed* (Cambridge: Cambridge University Press, 1994).

Wells, Bill, *Inward Migration of Skilled Labour to the UK*, IPPR Discussion Paper (London: Institute for Public Policy Research, 2001).

Winter-Ebner, Rudolf and Josef Zweimüller, 'Do Immigrants Displace Young Native Workers? The Austrian Experience', *Journal of Population Economics*, Vol. 12, No. 2, 1999, pp. 327–40.

Wolken, Simone, *Das Grundrecht auf Asyl als Gegenstand der Innen- und Rechtspolitik in der Bundesrepublik Deutschland* (Frankfurt am Main: Peter Lang, 1987).

Zincone, Giovanna, 'Immigration to Italy: Data and Policies', in F. Heckmann and W. Bosswick (eds), *Migration Policies: A Comparative Perspective* (Stuttgart: Enke, 1995), pp. 137–56.

Zincone, Giovanna, 'Italy – Main Features of Italian Immigration Flows', paper presented at the German Marshall Fund of the United States meeting on 'The Transatlantic Dialogue on Refugee and Asylum Policies', 16–17 October 2001.

Zolberg, Aristide R., Astri Suhrke and Sergio Aguayo, *Escape from Violence: Conflict and the Refugee Crisis in the Developing World: Beyond Progress and Development* (Oxford and New York: Oxford University Press, 1989).

# Index

Printed in the United States
131460LV00004B/17/P